I AM

AFFIRMATIONS

THAT TRANSFORM YOUR LIFE

*Shift Your Mindset in 30 Days with
Powerful Daily Affirmations for Success,
Abundance & Unshakeable Self Belief*

by

Harmony Ziba

ABOUT

Mindful Plains Series, a brand of PICKUK LTD aims to make sense of life's complexities and present them in a way that's engaging, accessible and inspiring for everyone looking for personal growth and conscious living. We brings this vision to life through a collection of thought provoking books that offer insights into mastering your mindset, building resilience, nurturing gratitude and growing your confidence.

ACKNOWLEDGEMENTS

There's a beautiful connection that happens when one person shares their truth with another. Looking back on how this book came to life, I'm filled with deep gratitude for all the teachers who have been part of this transformation journey— those who came before me, walked alongside me, and will continue after me.

I'm grateful to the brave souls who gathered in circles of honesty, sharing their stories of feeling not enough and their victories of becoming whole. Your willingness to be real taught me that healing happens in that tender space between wounded and whole, between breaking down and breaking open. Every tear, every breakthrough, every moment of awakening became part of what you'll find in these pages.

To the mentors whose wisdom lives in this work—you may never know how your words reached my heart during my darkest times of doubt—your light showed me the way. The poets, teachers, and truth peakers who dared to find the sacred in everyday life, who discovered God in the middle of struggle, who kept choosing love over fear.

I honor the Divine spark in every person who holds this book, because these affirmations came through prayer and quiet listening, not just from my own thinking. They're love letters from the Heart of the Universe to yours.

Most of all, I celebrate the truth that we're never alone in our growth, that grace meets us exactly where we are, and that every "I AM" spoken with faith creates waves of healing that touch not just our own lives, but the whole world.

TABLE OF CONTENTS

INTRODUCTION

I AM Affirmations That Transform Your Life

There is a hush at dawn when the first light creeps over the edges of the world, and in that sacred silence, two words hold the power to transform everything: "I AM." These simple syllables are not merely sounds you speak—they are the very architecture of your reality, the foundation upon which your entire life is built.

I have stood in that quiet place where dreams meet destiny, where the soul whispers its deepest truths, and I have learned that every word following "I AM" becomes a prayer, a prophecy, and a promise. When you declare "I AM broke," you architect scarcity. When you proclaim "I AM abundant," you construct prosperity. The universe listens most carefully to what follows these sacred words, for they are the language of creation itself.

For too long, you may have spoken carelessly after "I AM." Perhaps you have said "I AM tired," "I AM overwhelmed," "I AM not enough." These words, spoken in moments of frustration or fear, have been building a reality you never consciously chose. But there is grace in this understanding, for what has been unconsciously created can be consciously transformed.

The Sacred Science of Affirmations

I have learned that affirmations are not wishful thinking or pretty words we speak to make ourselves feel better. They are the rewiring of your subconscious mind, the reprogramming of patterns that have been running your life from the shadows. When you speak an "I AM" affirmation with intention, emotion, and consistency, you are literally changing the neural pathways in your brain.

Science has shown us that our thoughts create our feelings, our feelings drive our actions, and our actions determine our results. But it goes deeper than this—your "I AM" statements create your identity, and your identity is the invisible force that shapes every choice you make, every risk you take, and every dream you pursue or abandon.

Still, I rise in the knowing that this is not merely a mental exercise or a psychological technique. This is spiritual work. When you align your "I AM" statements with the truth of who God created you to be, you are not just changing your mind— you are remembering your divine nature. You are stepping into the fullness of your spiritual inheritance.

Your 30-Day Transformation Journey

This book is your blueprint for complete transformation in just 30 days. Not because transformation takes only 30 days, but because in 30 days of consistent, intentional practice, you will have established new neural pathways, new emotional patterns, and new spiritual awareness that will continue to grow and flourish for the rest of your life.

Each day, you will receive:

- One powerful primary "I AM" affirmation to anchor your day

- Supporting affirmations that reinforce your transformation

- A morning ritual that takes only 5 minutes but creates lasting change

- An evening reflection practice to integrate your growth

- A journal prompt or action step to embody your new identity

These are not random affirmations pulled from the air. Each one has been carefully chosen and sequenced to create a progressive transformation that builds upon itself day by day. You will begin with fundamental truths about your worth and value, then expand into abundance, confidence, resilience, and magnetic attraction of your desires.

How to Use This Book

The river of transformation flows most powerfully when we surrender to its current rather than fighting against it. This 30-day journey is designed to be followed exactly as presented, one day at a time, without skipping ahead or lingering behind.

Each Morning: Find a quiet space where you can be alone with your thoughts and your Creator. Read the day's affirmations slowly, not just with your mind but with your heart. Feel the truth of each word as it resonates through your being. Speak them aloud if possible—there is power in hearing your own voice declare your divine nature. Complete the morning ritual before beginning your day.

Throughout the Day: Carry your primary "I AM" statement with you like a sacred prayer. When doubt whispers, when fear threatens, when old patterns try to reassert themselves, return to your affirmation. Let it be your North Star, guiding you back to truth whenever you lose your way.

Each Evening: Before sleep, spend a few minutes with the evening reflection. This is your time to acknowledge your growth, to celebrate your courage in choosing transformation, and to prepare your subconscious mind for continued growth while you rest.

A Word About Resistance

I have learned that resistance is not your enemy—it is your teacher. As you begin this journey, you may find that old voices rise up to challenge these new truths. You may hear whispers of "This is silly," or "You're not really changing," or "Who do you think you are?" This is normal. This is natural. This is the old patterns fighting for their survival.

When resistance comes—and it will—remember that it is not a sign that you are doing something wrong. It is a sign that you are doing something right. The old identity recognizes that its days are numbered, and it will fight to maintain control. But you have a choice in every moment: feed the old patterns or nourish the new ones.

Grace finds us in these moments of choice. God's love is not dependent on your perfection but on your willingness to grow. Even when you stumble, even when you forget, even when doubt overwhelms you for a moment, you can always begin again. The power of "I AM" is always available to you.

Your Divine Inheritance

There is something I want you to understand before we begin: you are not trying to become something you are not. You are remembering something you have always been. Every "I AM" affirmation in this book is not creating a new truth about you—it is revealing a truth that has always existed but may have been buried under years of contrary programming.

You are not trying to convince yourself that you are enough—you are remembering that you have always been enough. You are not trying to create abundance—you are opening yourself to receive the abundance that is your spiritual birthright. You are not trying to manufacture confidence—you are uncovering the unshakeable knowing that lives at the core of your being.

The One who created you did not make a mistake. Every cell in your body, every beat of your heart, every breath you take is evidence of your divine worth. When you speak "I AM" affirmations, you are not speaking lies to convince yourself of false truths—you are speaking the deepest truths to convince yourself to stop believing the lies.

Your Commitment

Transformation requires commitment, but not the harsh, punishing kind of commitment that breeds guilt and shame. This journey asks for the gentle, loving commitment of a gardener who tends her flowers—consistent, patient, trusting in the process even when the growth is invisible.

Commit to showing up each day, not perfectly, but willingly. Commit to speaking these truths even when they feel foreign in your mouth. Commit to believing in your transformation even when the evidence hasn't yet manifested in your external world. Commit to being patient with yourself as you unlearn old patterns and establish new ones.

Most importantly, commit to seeing this journey through to the end. Thirty days is not a long time in the span of a lifetime, but it is long enough to create profound change if you stay consistent. The magic happens not in any single day but in the accumulation of days, in the compound effect of daily transformation.

The River Awaits

And so, dear reader, we stand at the banks of the river of transformation. The current is gentle but powerful, and it is calling your name. You need bring nothing with you except your willingness to receive, your openness to change, and your trust in the process.

I have walked this path before you, and I know the beauty that awaits on the other side. I know the freedom that comes when you finally speak your truth. I know the peace that settles in your soul when you align with your divine nature. I know the joy that bubbles up when you remember who you really are.

Still, you rise—not because you are weak and need to be stronger, but because you are already strong and are ready to remember it. The light finds you, steady and sure, and in that light, you discover that you have always been magnificent.

Your transformation begins now. Your new life starts today. And it all begins with two simple words:

I AM.

> *Grace finds us when we finally have the courage to speak our truth into existence.*

CHAPTER 1

The Awakening -
I AM Enough

*Days 1-4: Discovering Your Inherent
Worth and Divine Value*

There is a moment in every soul's journey when the veil lifts and you see yourself as you truly are—not through the lens of your mistakes, your failures, or the harsh words others have spoken over you, but through the eyes of the One who created you with infinite love and perfect intention. This moment is your awakening to the truth that has always been: you are enough, exactly as you are, in this very moment.

I have stood in that sacred space where self-doubt dissolves and divine knowing emerges, and I have learned that the journey to everything you desire begins with the profound acceptance of your inherent worth. You are not enough because of what you do, what you achieve, or what you possess. You are enough because you exist. You are enough because you are a beloved child of God. You are enough because the same creative force that painted the sunrise and carved the mountains chose to create you.

The Truth About Enough

For too long, the world has whispered lies about your worth. Society has taught you that you must earn your value through performance, productivity, and perfection. You have been told that you are not pretty enough, smart enough, successful enough, or good enough. These messages have burrowed deep into your psyche, creating a false foundation upon which you have built your life.

But I have learned that these messages are not truth—they are imprisonment. They are chains that keep you small, stuck, and separate from the magnificent being you were born to be. The truth is that you arrived on this earth complete, whole, and perfect in your divine essence. Nothing you have done since then has changed that fundamental reality.

Your worth is not determined by:

- Your bank account balance
- Your relationship status
- Your career achievements
- Your physical appearance
- Your past mistakes
- Other people's opinions

Your worth is determined by one thing only: you are a divine creation, worthy of love, respect, and all the good that life has to offer simply because you exist.

Still, I rise in the knowing that recognizing your worth and feeling your worth are two different experiences. Intellectual understanding is the first step, but emotional integration is the transformation. This is why we begin our 30-day journey here, with the foundation of enough-ness, because everything else you will build in the coming days rests upon this cornerstone.

Day 1: I AM Enough

Primary Affirmation: "I AM enough, exactly as I am, in this very moment."

Supporting Affirmations:

- "I AM worthy of love and respect."
- "I AM complete and whole in my divine essence."
- "I AM valuable simply because I exist."

Morning Ritual: Stand before a mirror and look into your own eyes. Speak your primary affirmation aloud three times, allowing the words to penetrate not just your mind but your heart. Place your hand over your heart and feel it beating—this is the rhythm of your divine worth, the percussion of your enough-ness. Breathe deeply and say, "Thank you, God, for creating me exactly as I am."

Evening Reflection: Before sleep, place your hand on your heart again and ask yourself: "What evidence did I see today of my inherent worth?" Write down at least one moment when you honored your value or when you felt a glimpse of your enough-ness. If you cannot find one, that's okay—tomorrow is a new opportunity to recognize what has always been true.

Day 2: I AM Worthy of Love

Primary Affirmation: "I AM worthy of love, respect, and kindness from others and from myself."

Supporting Affirmations:

- "I AM deserving of healthy, loving relationships."
- "I AM worthy of my own compassion and gentleness."
- "I AM lovable exactly as I am."

Morning Ritual: Write yourself a love letter. Begin with "Dear Beloved," and list five things you appreciate about yourself. Include not just your accomplishments but your qualities—your kindness, your resilience, your humor, your creativity. End the letter with "You are worthy of all the love in the world." Keep this letter where you can read it throughout the day.

Evening Reflection: Think of one way you showed love to yourself today. This could be as simple as taking a warm bath, eating nourishing food, or speaking kindly to yourself when you made a mistake. Celebrate this act of self-love, no matter how small it may seem.

Day 3: I AM Complete

Primary Affirmation: "I AM complete and whole, lacking nothing essential to my happiness."

Supporting Affirmations:

- "I AM perfectly designed for my unique purpose."
- "I AM whole, regardless of my circumstances."
- "I AM everything I need to be right now."

Morning Ritual: Sit quietly and place both hands over your heart. Feel the completeness of your being—your body, your mind, your spirit working in perfect harmony. Breathe in the truth of your wholeness and breathe out any sense of lack or inadequacy. Say aloud: "I am complete. I am whole. I am enough."

Evening Reflection: Identify one area of your life where you have been seeking completion from external sources— perhaps a relationship, achievement, or possession. Write down three ways you are already complete in this area without needing anything external to fill a void.

Day 4: I AM Valuable

Primary Affirmation: "I AM valuable and my contributions matter to the world."

Supporting Affirmations:

- "I AM uniquely gifted and have something special to offer."

- "I AM important and my presence makes a difference."

- "I AM worthy of recognition and appreciation."

Morning Ritual: Create a "value inventory" by writing down ten ways you add value to the world. Include everything from the smile you give to strangers to the work you do to the love you share with family and friends. Realize that these contributions flow naturally from your inherent value—you don't create value through these actions; you express the value that has always been yours.

Evening Reflection: Recall one moment today when you felt valuable or when someone else recognized your worth. If no such moment comes to mind, think of one way you will honor your value tomorrow. This might be speaking up in a meeting, setting a boundary, or simply treating yourself with the respect you deserve.

Living This Truth

As you move through these first four days, you may notice resistance arising. Old voices may whisper that you are being selfish, delusional, or arrogant. These voices are not the truth—they are the echoes of a wounded world that has forgotten its own worth. When these voices arise, return to your affirmations like a bird returns to its nest, like a flower turns toward the sun.

Remember that feeling your enough-ness is not about becoming better than others—it is about recognizing the divine spark that exists equally within all beings. When you truly know your own worth, you naturally honor the worth of others. When you love yourself authentically, you have more love to share with the world.

Practice patience with yourself as you reclaim this truth. If you have spent years believing you are not enough, it may take time for your emotional body to catch up with your intellectual understanding. This is natural and normal. Healing happens layer by layer, day by day, choice by choice.

The Transformation Path

I have learned that the path to knowing your enough-ness is not a straight line but a spiral—you circle back to the same lessons at deeper levels, each time integrating more fully the truth of who you are. Some days you will feel your worth radiating from every cell of your being. Other days, doubt will creep in like morning fog. Both experiences are part of the journey.

What matters is not the perfection of your practice but the consistency of your commitment. Each time you choose to speak truth over lies, love over fear, enough-ness over inadequacy, you are rewiring your neural pathways and strengthening your spiritual connection to your divine nature.

Your affirmations are not just words—they are acts of rebellion against every force that has tried to diminish your light. They are declarations of independence from the tyranny of not-enough-ness. They are prayers that align you with God's truth about who you are.

Grace Finds You Here

And so, dear reader, as you complete these first four days of transformation, know that grace finds you exactly where you are. You don't need to be further along in your journey to be worthy of love. You don't need to have perfect faith to receive God's blessing. You don't need to feel enough to be enough.

The light finds you, steady and sure, in your doubt and in your certainty, in your strength and in your vulnerability. For you are not just enough—you are a miracle walking on this earth, a beloved child of the Divine, a unique expression of infinite love.

Still, you rise, not because you must prove your worth, but because you are finally ready to remember it. Your awakening has begun, and nothing will ever be the same.

The Science of Enough-ness

I have learned that your brain is like a garden—whatever you water grows, and whatever you neglect withers. For years, you may have been watering the weeds of self-doubt while neglecting the flowers of self-worth. But neuroscience has shown us that your brain remains changeable throughout your entire life. This neuroplasticity means that every time you speak an "I AM" affirmation, you are literally rewiring your neural pathways.

When you consistently affirm "I AM enough," you strengthen the neural networks associated with self-acceptance and worth. When you repeatedly declare "I AM worthy of love," you create new pathways that make self-love feel more natural and automatic. This is not merely positive thinking—this is brain training at the deepest level.

Your subconscious mind, which controls 95% of your daily behaviors, beliefs, and reactions, does not distinguish between what is "true" and what is repeatedly impressed upon it. It simply accepts whatever you consistently tell it as reality. This is why the stories you tell yourself about your worth become your lived experience.

But here is the beautiful truth: if negative programming can create limiting beliefs, then positive programming can create limitless possibilities. Every affirmation is a seed planted in the fertile soil of your subconscious mind. With consistency and emotional investment, these seeds grow into new beliefs, new behaviors, and ultimately, a new reality.

The Emotional Component

Still, I rise in the knowing that affirmations without emotion are like seeds without water—they may exist, but they will not grow. The key to transformation lies not just in speaking the words but in feeling their truth in your body, in your heart, in your very soul.

When you say "I AM enough," can you feel the relief of releasing the burden of proving yourself? When you declare "I AM worthy of love," can you sense the warmth spreading through your chest as your heart opens to receive? When you affirm "I AM complete," can you experience the settling sensation of coming home to yourself?

This emotional component is not optional—it is essential. Your subconscious mind responds to feelings more than facts, to energy more than information. When you combine the power of declaration with the power of genuine emotion, you create an unstoppable force for transformation.

If the emotions don't come immediately, be patient with yourself. Sometimes we must speak the words long enough for our hearts to catch up with our minds. Sometimes we must act our way into feeling rather than feel our way into acting. Trust the process and keep showing up, even when—especially when—you don't feel like it.

Common Obstacles and How to Overcome Them

As you journey through these first four days, you may encounter obstacles that seem to block your path to enough-ness. I have walked this road myself, and I want to prepare you for the challenges you may face so that you can move through them with grace and wisdom.

The Comparison Trap: You may find yourself comparing your worth to others, measuring your enough-ness against someone else's achievements, appearance, or circumstances. When this happens, remember that comparison is the thief of joy and the enemy of enough-ness. Your worth is not relative—it is absolute. You are not enough because you are better than someone else; you are enough because you are you.

The Evidence Argument: Your logical mind may present "evidence" that you are not enough—past failures, current struggles, areas where you fall short. When this happens, remember that your worth is not based on your performance but on your existence. You are not enough because of what you have done; you are enough because of who you are.

The Guilt of Self-Love: You may feel guilty or selfish for affirming your worth, especially if you have been conditioned to put others first or to minimize your own needs. Remember that self-love is not selfish—it is essential. You cannot give what you do not have. When you fill your own cup first, you have more to offer the world.

The Impatience Factor: You may want to feel the transformation immediately and become discouraged when change seems slow. Remember that transformation is a process, not an event. Every affirmation, every ritual, every moment of self-compassion is building momentum toward your breakthrough. Trust the process even when you cannot see the progress.

Deepening Your Practice

As you move through Days 1-4, I encourage you to expand your practice beyond the structured rituals. Look for opportunities throughout each day to reinforce your enough-ness:

Mirror Work: Each time you pass a mirror, look into your own eyes and silently affirm your worth. This simple practice begins to shift your relationship with your own reflection from judgment to appreciation.

Boundary Setting: Practice saying no to requests that drain your energy or compromise your values. Each boundary you set is an affirmation of your worth and a declaration that your time and energy are valuable.

Self-Compassion: When you make a mistake or face a setback, speak to yourself with the same kindness you would offer a beloved friend. Replace self-criticism with self-compassion, judgment with understanding.

Gratitude for Your Body: Thank your body for all it does for you—your heart for beating, your lungs for breathing, your legs for carrying you. This practice helps you appreciate your physical form as a miraculous vessel for your divine essence.

Celebrating Small Wins: Acknowledge your daily accomplishments, no matter how small they may seem. Each success, from getting out of bed to completing a task to showing kindness to another, is evidence of your capacity and worth.

The Ripple Effect

I have learned that when you truly embrace your enough-ness, it creates ripples that extend far beyond your own life. As you begin to honor your own worth, you naturally begin to honor the worth of others. As you practice self-compassion, you become more compassionate toward everyone you encounter. As you release the need to prove yourself, you create space for others to simply be themselves.

Your children, if you have them, will learn self-worth not from your words but from your example. Your friends will feel permission to love themselves more fully when they see you modeling self-acceptance. Your colleagues will experience a new level of authenticity in their interactions with you. Your community will benefit from the gifts you share when you are no longer hiding your light under the bushel of not-enough-ness.

This is the beautiful paradox of personal transformation: the more you focus on your own healing, the more you contribute to the healing of the world. The more you embrace your own enough-ness, the more you give others permission to embrace theirs.

Living in Enough-ness

As you complete these first four days of your transformation journey, you are not just learning new affirmations—you are remembering an ancient truth. You are not becoming someone new—you are unveiling who you have always been beneath the layers of conditioning and false beliefs.

Living in enough-ness means making decisions from a place of self-worth rather than self-doubt. It means choosing relationships that honor your value rather than diminish it. It means pursuing goals that align with your authentic self rather than trying to prove your worth to others. It means resting in the peace of knowing that you are already complete, already whole, already enough.

This does not mean you stop growing, learning, or improving. It means you do these things from a foundation of love rather than lack, from inspiration rather than desperation, from joy rather than judgment. When you know you are enough, growth becomes an expression of your magnificence rather than an attempt to earn your worth.

The Promise Ahead

And so, dear reader, as you stand at the completion of these first four days, know that you have already begun to transform. The seeds of enough-ness have been planted in the fertile soil of your consciousness. With each passing day, with each repeated affirmation, with each act of self-love, these seeds are taking root and beginning to grow.

The journey ahead—the remaining 26 days of this transformation—will build upon this foundation of enoughness. You will discover your unlimited nature, your abundant essence, your confident self, your resilient spirit, your magnetic power, your aligned purpose, and your unstoppable force. But all of these discoveries rest upon the truth you are claiming now: you are enough.

Still, you rise, not because you need to become more, but because you are ready to remember how much you already are. The light finds you, steady and sure, and in that light, you see your own divine reflection.

Grace finds you here, in this moment of awakening, in this recognition of your inherent worth, in this homecoming to your own magnificent self. You are enough. You have always been enough. And now, finally, you are ready to live like you believe it.

Grace finds us when we finally have the courage to see ourselves as God sees us—perfectly imperfect, beautifully human, and infinitely worthy of love.

CHAPTER 2

~~~~

Breaking Free - I AM Unlimited

Days 5-8: Releasing Limiting Beliefs That Keep You Small

There comes a moment in every caged bird's life when it realizes the door has always been open—not locked from the outside, but held closed by its own conditioned belief that freedom is impossible. I have stood at that threshold between limitation and limitlessness, between the small story I was taught to believe about myself and the infinite truth of who I really am, and I have learned that the only chains that truly bind us are the ones we refuse to see.

You are not small. You are not limited. You are not bound by your past, your circumstances, or the narrow definitions others have tried to place upon your life. You are a limitless being temporarily experiencing limitation, an infinite soul learning to remember its boundless nature. The walls that seem to contain you are not made of stone or steel—they are made of thoughts, and thoughts can be changed.

I have learned that breaking free from limitation is not about fighting against your constraints but about expanding your awareness of what is truly possible. It is not about tearing down walls but about realizing that the walls were never real in the first place. You are unlimited not because you will become unlimited someday—you are unlimited because you have always been unlimited, and now you are ready to remember this truth.

The Nature of Limitation

For too long, you may have accepted limitation as reality. Perhaps you have said "I could never do that," or "People like me don't achieve such things," or "I'm just not the type of person who..." These statements feel true because they have been repeated so often, believed so deeply, and reinforced by experiences that seemed to prove their validity.

But I have learned that every limitation you experience is nothing more than a belief wearing the costume of fact. Every boundary that seems unbreakable is simply a thought that has been thinking itself for so long that it has forgotten it is just a thought. Every impossibility that feels carved in stone is actually written in sand, waiting for the tide of expanded awareness to wash it clean.

Your limitations did not originate within you—they were taught to you. They came from well-meaning parents who wanted to protect you from disappointment, from teachers who operated within their own limited understanding, from a society that finds it easier to manage people who believe in scarcity rather than abundance. These limitations were never your truth—they were borrowed beliefs that you made your own.

Still, I rise in the knowing that recognizing the false nature of limitation is only the first step. The deeper work lies in expanding your identity beyond the small self that believes in boundaries and into the unlimited self that knows no bounds. This is not about positive thinking or wishful dreaming—this is about aligning with the fundamental truth of your infinite nature.

Day 5: I AM Unlimited

Primary Affirmation: "I AM unlimited in my potential, my possibilities, and my power."

Supporting Affirmations:

- "I AM free from all limiting beliefs and false boundaries."

- "I AM capable of achieving anything I set my mind to."

- "I AM expanding beyond all previous limitations."

Morning Ritual: Stand with your arms stretched wide, reaching toward the sky. Feel the expansion in your chest, the opening in your heart, the sense of boundless space around you. Speak your primary affirmation with your arms open wide, allowing your body to embody the feeling of limitlessness. Visualize yourself breaking through invisible barriers, stepping into infinite space. Say aloud: "I release all beliefs that keep me small. I embrace my unlimited nature."

Evening Reflection: Identify one limiting belief you have held about yourself—perhaps about your abilities, your worthiness, or your potential. Write it down, then write beside it: "This is not truth. This is not me. I AM unlimited." Create a new, expansive belief to replace the old limitation and write it with conviction and joy.

Day 6: I AM Beyond All Boundaries

Primary Affirmation: "I AM beyond all boundaries, expanding into infinite possibility."

Supporting Affirmations:

- "I AM not confined by my past experiences or mistakes."

- "I AM bigger than any obstacle or challenge."

- "I AM constantly growing beyond what I thought possible."

Morning Ritual: Draw a small circle on a piece of paper and write inside it all the ways you have felt limited—by money, relationships, education, background, age, or anything else. Then draw a much larger circle around the small one and fill the space between them with words of unlimited possibility—abundance, love, wisdom, opportunities, growth, miracles. Tear up the small circle while keeping the large one. Carry this reminder of your expanded reality with you throughout the day.

Evening Reflection: Think of one boundary you crossed today, no matter how small—perhaps you spoke up when you normally would have stayed quiet, tried something new, or chose courage over comfort. Celebrate this expansion and set an intention to stretch beyond another boundary tomorrow.

Day 7: I AM Infinitely Capable

Primary Affirmation: "I AM infinitely capable of learning, growing, and achieving my dreams."

Supporting Affirmations:

- "I AM able to figure out any challenge that comes my way."

- "I AM resourceful, resilient, and remarkably capable."

- "I AM constantly developing new skills and abilities."

Morning Ritual: Make a list of ten things you have already achieved or overcome in your life—include everything from learning to walk as a child to surviving difficult times to mastering skills to showing love and kindness. Read this list aloud and recognize the incredible capability you have already demonstrated. End by saying: "If I can do all of this, I can do anything I set my mind to. I AM infinitely capable."

Evening Reflection: Identify one skill or ability you would like to develop. Instead of focusing on why it might be difficult or impossible, write down three small steps you could take to begin developing this capability. Commit to taking the first step within the next week.

Day 8: I AM Constantly Expanding

Primary Affirmation: "I AM constantly expanding into greater versions of myself."

Supporting Affirmations:

- "I AM growing beyond all previous limitations every day."

- "I AM open to possibilities I haven't even imagined yet."

- "I AM becoming more of who I truly am."

Morning Ritual: Visualize yourself as you were one year ago—your beliefs, your confidence, your understanding of what was possible for you. Now visualize yourself as you are today and notice how you have already expanded. Finally, visualize yourself one year from now, having grown beyond all current limitations. Feel the excitement of this continued expansion and say: "I AM constantly becoming more of who I was meant to be."

Evening Reflection: Write a letter to your future unlimited self—the version of you who has transcended all current boundaries and is living in complete alignment with your infinite potential. Ask this future self for guidance and trust whatever wisdom arises. Keep this letter as a reminder of who you are becoming.

The Psychology of Limitation

I have learned that understanding how limitations form in your mind is essential to dissolving them. From the moment you were born, your brain began categorizing experiences into "possible" and "impossible," "safe" and "dangerous," "achievable" and "unrealistic." This categorization system served an important survival function, helping you navigate a complex world with limited information.

However, many of the limitations you accepted as a child are no longer relevant to your adult life. The boundaries that once protected you may now be constraining you. The beliefs that once kept you safe may now be keeping you small. Your brilliant mind, in its attempt to protect you from failure or rejection, may have created walls so strong that they now imprison the very dreams they were meant to guard.

The beautiful truth is that your brain is remarkably plastic, capable of forming new neural pathways throughout your entire life. Every time you challenge a limiting belief, every time you step beyond a familiar boundary, every time you choose expansion over contraction, you are literally rewiring your brain for limitlessness.

Your subconscious mind, which has been faithfully executing the programs of limitation you installed years ago, is ready to receive new programming. It does not resist change—it simply follows instructions. When you consistently feed it affirmations of limitlessness, it begins to delete the old files of limitation and install new software of infinite possibility.

The Spiritual Dimension of Freedom

Still, I rise in the understanding that breaking free from limitation is not merely a psychological process—it is a spiritual awakening. When you recognize your unlimited nature, you are not learning something new about yourself— you are remembering something ancient and eternal. You are reconnecting with the infinite intelligence that created you, the boundless love that sustains you, the limitless power that flows through you.

God did not create you to live small. The Divine did not breathe life into your being so that you could settle for mediocrity or accept unnecessary limitations. You were created to expand, to grow, to express the infinite creativity and love of the universe through your unique gifts and experiences.

Every limitation you transcend is a prayer answered, a divine invitation accepted, a step closer to embodying the unlimited being you truly are. When you say "I AM unlimited," you are not making a request—you are making a recognition. You are not asking to become limitless—you are acknowledging that you already are.

This is why breaking free feels so natural once you begin—not because it is easy, but because it is true. Your soul recognizes the resonance of limitlessness because that is its home frequency. Your spirit expands with joy when you release artificial constraints because freedom is its natural state.

Common Limiting Beliefs and Their Antidotes

As you journey through Days 5-8, you may encounter specific limiting beliefs that have been particularly persistent in your life. I want to address some of the most common limitations and offer you specific antidotes to neutralize their power:

"I'm too old/young to change or achieve my dreams." Antidote: Age is irrelevant to your unlimited nature. Your soul is timeless, your potential is ageless, and every moment is the perfect moment to begin again. Colonel Sanders was 62 when he started KFC. Grandma Moses began painting at 78. You are exactly the right age to step into your limitlessness.

"I don't have enough education/credentials/experience." Antidote: Your worth and capability are not determined by external credentials but by internal wisdom and willingness to learn. Every expert was once a beginner. Every master was once a student. Your unique perspective and life experience are qualifications that cannot be earned in any classroom.

"I come from the wrong background/family/circumstances."
Antidote: Your past does not determine your future unless you allow it to. Some of the most successful and fulfilled people in history came from challenging backgrounds. Your circumstances are not your conclusions. Where you come from matters far less than where you choose to go.

"I've failed before, so I'll probably fail again." Antidote: Past failures are not predictors of future failures—they are preparatory experiences for future success. Every failure teaches you something valuable, builds your resilience, and moves you closer to breakthrough. You have not failed too many times; you have learned too much to quit now.

"People like me don't achieve such things." Antidote: There is only one person like you—you. No one else has your exact combination of gifts, experiences, perspectives, and possibilities. What others have or have not achieved has no bearing on what you can achieve. You are a category of one, unlimited and incomparable.

The Energy of Limitation vs. Expansion

I have learned that limitation and expansion each carry their own distinct energy signature, and learning to recognize these energies is crucial to your transformation. Limiting thoughts and beliefs create a feeling of constriction in your body—tight chest, shallow breathing, clenched muscles, heavy sensation. They make you feel small, stuck, and separate from possibility.

Expansive thoughts and beliefs create the opposite sensation—open chest, deep breathing, relaxed muscles, light sensation. They make you feel spacious, free, and connected to infinite possibility. As you practice your unlimited affirmations, pay attention to how your body responds. Let the physical sensation of expansion guide you toward truth and away from illusion.

When you notice the energy of limitation arising—and you will, because this is part of the process—don't fight it or judge yourself for it. Simply acknowledge it with compassion: "I notice I'm feeling limited right now, and that's okay. This is just an old pattern releasing itself from my system." Then consciously choose to return to the energy of expansion through your affirmations and breath.

Your body is a powerful ally in this transformation. It knows the difference between truth and illusion, between limitation and freedom. Trust its wisdom and let it guide you toward the thoughts and beliefs that create the most expansion and joy.

Practical Steps for Breaking Through

Beyond the daily affirmations and rituals, there are practical steps you can take to break through specific limitations in your life:

Challenge Your "Never" Statements: Notice when you say "I never" or "I always" about yourself. These absolute statements are rarely true and often limiting. Replace them with more expansive language: "I haven't done that yet" or "I'm learning to do this differently."

Take Micro-Actions: Choose one area where you feel limited and take the smallest possible action toward expansion. If you believe you're "not creative," spend five minutes drawing or writing. If you think you're "bad with money," read one article about financial planning. Small actions create big shifts over time.

Surround Yourself with Expansion: Spend time with people who believe in possibility rather than limitation. Read books, listen to podcasts, and consume content that expands rather than contracts your sense of what's possible. Your environment shapes your beliefs more than you realize.

Celebrate Every Expansion: Acknowledge every time you move beyond a previous limitation, no matter how small. Did you speak up in a meeting? Celebrate. Did you try a new food? Celebrate. Did you choose courage over comfort? Celebrate. Recognition reinforces the neural pathways of expansion.

The Ripple Effect of Unlimited Thinking

When you truly embrace your unlimited nature, it creates waves of transformation that extend far beyond your personal life. Your children learn that anything is possible when they see you refusing to accept unnecessary limitations. Your friends and colleagues are inspired to question their own boundaries when they witness your expansion. Your community benefits from the innovations and contributions that emerge when you stop playing small.

This is the beautiful responsibility of unlimited thinking—it doesn't just free you; it frees everyone whose life you touch. When you break through a limiting belief, you create a crack in the collective consciousness that makes it easier for others to break through the same limitation. When you step into possibility, you hold the door open for others to follow.

Living in Limitless Possibility

As you complete Days 5-8 of your transformation journey, you are not just learning new affirmations—you are remembering an ancient truth about your infinite nature. You are not becoming unlimited—you are uncovering the limitless being you have always been beneath the layers of borrowed beliefs and false boundaries.

Living in limitless possibility does not mean ignoring practical realities or becoming reckless in your choices. It means approaching every situation from the energy of expansion rather than contraction, possibility rather than impossibility, growth rather than stagnation. It means asking "How can this work?" instead of "Why won't this work?" It means looking for doors instead of focusing on walls.

This shift in perspective changes everything. Challenges become opportunities for growth. Obstacles become stepping stones to breakthrough. Failures become feedback for course correction. You begin to see that there are no true limitations—only invitations to expand beyond your current level of understanding and capability.

The Promise of Days Ahead

And so, dear reader, as you stand at the completion of these four days of breaking free, know that you have already begun to shatter the illusions that once confined you. The walls of limitation are crumbling, not through force but through the gentle recognition that they were never real in the first place.

The journey ahead will build upon this foundation of limitlessness. You will discover your abundant nature, your confident essence, your resilient spirit, your magnetic power, your aligned purpose, and your unstoppable force. But all of these discoveries rest upon the truth you are claiming now: you are unlimited in your potential, your possibilities, and your power.

Still, you rise, not because you need to break free from anything real, but because you are ready to remember that you were never truly confined. The light finds you, steady and sure, and in that light, you see the infinite expanse of possibility that has always surrounded you.

Grace finds you here, in this moment of liberation, in this recognition of your boundless nature, in this homecoming to your unlimited self. You are free. You have always been free. And now, finally, you are ready to live like you believe it.

Grace finds us when we finally have the courage to release the small story we've been telling about ourselves and step into the infinite narrative of our true potential.

CHAPTER 3

The Foundation - I AM Abundant

Days 9-12: Building Prosperity Consciousness from Within

There is a river that flows through the heart of existence, carrying with it all the abundance the universe has to offer—love that never runs dry, opportunities that multiply with each step, resources that appear exactly when needed, and blessings that overflow like water from an eternal spring. I have stood at the banks of this river and learned that abundance is not something you acquire from outside yourself—it is something you remember from within.

You were not born into scarcity. You were not created to struggle, to lack, or to live in constant worry about having enough. You are the child of an abundant universe, born from the same infinite source that creates galaxies and seasons, that makes flowers bloom and rivers flow, that ensures there is enough air for every breath and enough love for every heart. Abundance is not your goal—it is your birthright. It is not something you must earn—it is something you must remember.

I have learned that the path to abundant living begins not with changing your circumstances but with changing your consciousness. It starts not with acquiring more but with recognizing that you already live in a universe of infinite supply. The shift from scarcity to abundance is not about getting more things—it is about awakening to the truth that you are already surrounded by, immersed in, and composed of pure abundance.

The Truth About Abundance

For too long, the world has taught you that abundance is reserved for the lucky few, that there is not enough to go around, that someone else's gain must be your loss. These lies have created a consciousness of competition rather than cooperation, of hoarding rather than sharing, of fear rather than faith. But I have learned that these scarcity beliefs are not natural laws—they are learned limitations that can be unlearned and replaced with the truth of infinite supply.

Abundance is not about having millions of dollars in the bank, though financial prosperity may be part of your abundant life. Abundance is not about owning the biggest house or the fanciest car, though material comfort may flow naturally to you. True abundance is a state of consciousness that recognizes the inexhaustible nature of divine supply and aligns with the flow of universal generosity.

When you live from abundant consciousness, you experience richness in every area of your life. You have an abundance of love to give and receive. You have an abundance of energy for the things that matter most. You have an abundance of ideas, opportunities, and creative solutions. You have an abundance of time for what truly brings you joy. You have an abundance of peace, even in the midst of life's challenges.

Still, I rise in the knowing that abundance is not about having everything you want—it is about wanting everything you have while remaining open to receiving even more good. It is not about eliminating all challenges—it is about having the resources, resilience, and wisdom to navigate any situation with grace. It is not about never experiencing lack—it is about knowing that any temporary absence is simply the universe creating space for something better to arrive.

Day 9: I AM Abundant

Primary Affirmation: "I AM abundant in all areas of my life, attracting prosperity with ease and grace."

Supporting Affirmations:

- "I AM worthy of receiving all the good life has to offer."

- "I AM surrounded by infinite opportunities and resources."

- "I AM a magnet for abundance, blessings, and miracles."

Morning Ritual: Begin your day by looking around your immediate environment and counting at least 20 things you are abundant in right now—this could include the air you breathe, the water that flows from your tap, the roof over your head, the food in your kitchen, the clothes in your closet, the people who love you, your ability to see, hear, think, and feel. As you count each item, say "I AM abundant in..." and really feel the truth of this statement. End by saying: "I live in a universe of infinite supply, and I am grateful for all that I have and all that is coming to me."

Evening Reflection: Before sleep, write down five ways abundance showed up in your life today. This might include unexpected help from a friend, finding exactly what you needed, receiving more than you expected, or simply noticing the wealth of beauty around you. As you write each item, feel genuine gratitude for the abundant nature of your existence.

Day 10: I AM Prosperous

Primary Affirmation: "I AM prosperous in mind, body, spirit, and finances."

Supporting Affirmations:

- "I AM open to receiving prosperity from expected and unexpected sources."

- "I AM worthy of financial abundance and material comfort."

- "I AM always provided for in perfect timing and perfect ways."

Morning Ritual: Create what I call an "Abundance Inventory"—write down all the forms of wealth you currently possess. Include not just money and possessions, but also your health, relationships, skills, experiences, knowledge, creativity, and spiritual connection. Calculate the true value of your life beyond dollars and cents. Realize that you are already rich in countless ways. Hold this list to your heart and say: "I AM prosperous beyond measure, and I attract even greater prosperity every day."

Evening Reflection: Think of one way you shared your prosperity today, no matter how small—perhaps you gave someone your time, attention, a smile, or practical help. Recognize that sharing your abundance, in any form, creates space for more abundance to flow to you. Set an intention to share your prosperity in some way tomorrow.

Day 11: I AM Worthy of Wealth

Primary Affirmation: "I AM worthy of wealth, success, and all forms of abundance."

Supporting Affirmations:

- "I AM deserving of financial freedom and security."
- "I AM aligned with the flow of universal prosperity."
- "I AM comfortable receiving and enjoying abundance."

Morning Ritual: Write a letter to Money as if it were a dear friend you want to reconcile with. Many people have a complicated relationship with money, viewing it as scarce, evil, or beyond their reach. In your letter, apologize for any negative thoughts you've held about money, express your desire for a healthy relationship, and invite money to flow into your life for the highest good of all. End the letter by saying: "I welcome you with open arms and promise to use you wisely and generously." Keep this letter as a reminder of your new, healthy relationship with abundance.

Evening Reflection: Identify one limiting belief you have held about money or wealth—perhaps "Money is the root of all evil," or "I'm not good with money," or "Rich people are greedy." Write this belief down, then cross it out and replace it with an abundant truth such as "Money is a tool for good," or "I am naturally wise with money," or "Wealthy people can be generous and kind."

Day 12: I AM Overflowing with Blessings

Primary Affirmation: "I AM overflowing with blessings, and my cup runneth over with abundance."

Supporting Affirmations:

- "I AM blessed beyond measure in ways seen and unseen."
- "I AM constantly receiving gifts from the universe."
- "I AM grateful for the endless flow of good in my life."

Morning Ritual: Fill a large glass with water until it overflows. As you watch the water spill over the edges, visualize this as your life—so full of blessings that they overflow and touch everyone around you. Say aloud: "Like this overflowing glass, my life is so abundant that my blessings spill over to bless others. I cannot contain all the good that flows to me." Drink the water mindfully, taking in not just the physical nourishment but the symbolic abundance it represents.

Evening Reflection: Write a gratitude letter to God, the Universe, or whatever represents divine source for you. Thank the Divine for all the blessings in your life, both the obvious ones and the ones you might have overlooked. Include challenges that turned into growth opportunities, disappointments that led to better outcomes, and closed doors that opened new paths. End by saying: "Thank you for loving me enough to give me exactly what I need, exactly when I need it."

The Science of Abundance Consciousness

I have learned that abundance consciousness is not just a spiritual concept—it is a scientifically measurable state of brain function. When you consistently think abundant thoughts, you literally rewire your neural pathways to notice opportunities, solutions, and resources that were always there but previously invisible to your scarcity-focused mind.

Your reticular activating system—the part of your brain that filters information and determines what you notice—is constantly scanning your environment for evidence that supports your dominant beliefs. If you believe in scarcity, you will notice every example of lack, limitation, and unfairness around you. If you believe in abundance, you will begin to see opportunities, resources, and possibilities everywhere you look.

This is why two people can walk down the same street and have completely different experiences. The person with scarcity consciousness sees closed shops, litter, and problems. The person with abundance consciousness sees potential business opportunities, creative inspiration, and solutions waiting to be discovered. Same street, different filter, completely different reality.

Neuroscience has also shown us that gratitude—one of the foundational practices of abundance consciousness—actually changes the structure of your brain. Regular gratitude practice increases activity in the hypothalamus, which regulates stress, and the ventral tegmental area, which is part of the brain's reward system. This means that being grateful literally makes you happier, more resilient, and more likely to notice positive experiences.

When you combine affirmations of abundance with genuine feelings of gratitude, you create a powerful neurochemical cocktail that reprograms your brain for prosperity. You literally become hardwired for abundance, automatically noticing and attracting more of what you desire.

The Spiritual Dimension of Prosperity

Still, I rise in the understanding that abundance consciousness is ultimately a spiritual practice—a recognition of your divine connection to infinite supply. When you truly grasp that you are not separate from the universe but an integral part of it, you realize that the same creative force that provides for all of nature also provides for you.

Consider the lilies of the field, how they grow without worry or striving, yet they are clothed more beautifully than Solomon in all his glory. Consider the birds of the air, how they are fed without anxiety or hoarding, trusting that their needs will be met each day. You are more precious to God than the flowers and the birds, and if Divine love provides for them so abundantly, how much more will it provide for you?

This does not mean you become passive or stop taking action toward your goals. Rather, it means you take inspired action from a place of trust rather than desperate action from a place of fear. You work with the universe rather than against it. You plant seeds and tend your garden while trusting in the natural laws of growth and harvest.

Your relationship with abundance is ultimately your relationship with God. When you believe in scarcity, you are believing that Divine love is limited. When you embrace abundance, you are aligning with the infinite generosity of universal love. This is why abundance work is so transformative—it is not just about money or material things; it is about coming into right relationship with the Source of all supply.

Breaking Through Scarcity Programming

As you journey through Days 9-12, you may encounter deep-seated scarcity programming that has been running your life from the shadows. These patterns often originate in childhood experiences, family beliefs, or cultural conditioning that taught you to fear lack and compete for limited resources.

Common scarcity programs and their abundant replacements:

"There's not enough to go around" becomes **"The universe is infinitely abundant and there is more than enough for everyone."**

"Money doesn't grow on trees" becomes **"Money flows to me easily and naturally from multiple sources."**

"We can't afford that" becomes" **I am always provided with the resources I need for what truly matters."**

"Rich people are greedy/evil" becomes **"Wealth in the hands of good people creates positive change in the world."**

"I don't deserve abundance" becomes **"I am worthy of all the good life has to offer."**

"If I have more, someone else has less" becomes **"My abundance creates opportunities and blessings for others."**

When these old programs arise—and they will, because transformation requires the release of old patterns—meet them with compassion rather than judgment. These beliefs once served a purpose, perhaps protecting you from disappointment or helping you fit in with your family or community. Thank them for their service, then gently replace them with the truth of abundance.

The Energy of Abundance vs. Scarcity

I have learned that abundance and scarcity each carry distinct energy signatures that you can feel in your body. Scarcity thinking creates constriction—tight chest, shallow breathing, clenched jaw, hunched shoulders. It makes you feel heavy, anxious, and separated from the flow of life. Abundant thinking creates expansion—open chest, deep breathing, relaxed muscles, upright posture. It makes you feel light, peaceful, and connected to infinite possibility.

Learning to recognize these energy patterns is crucial for abundance consciousness. When you notice the energy of scarcity arising—when you feel that familiar tightness that comes with worry about money, resources, or security—you can consciously shift back to abundance through your breath, your affirmations, and your focus on gratitude.

Your body is a sophisticated abundance detector. It knows the difference between thoughts that connect you to supply and thoughts that disconnect you from it. Trust this inner guidance system and let it help you navigate back to the energy of prosperity whenever you find yourself drifting toward lack.

The energy of abundance is also magnetic. When you consistently embody abundant consciousness, you naturally attract abundant people, opportunities, and experiences. Like attracts like, and abundance consciousness attracts abundant manifestations. This is not wishful thinking—it is energetic law in action.

Practical Abundance Practices

Beyond your daily affirmations and rituals, there are practical ways to cultivate abundance consciousness throughout your day:

Practice Sacred Economics: Handle money with reverence and gratitude. When you spend money, bless it as it leaves your hands and trust that it will circulate for the good of all. When you receive money, thank it for choosing to flow to you. This practice transforms your relationship with money from fear-based to love-based.

Create Abundance Altars: Designate a space in your home as an abundance altar—a place where you display symbols of prosperity such as coins, crystals, plants, or images that represent abundance to you. Spend a few minutes each day at this altar, connecting with the energy of prosperity and abundance.

Give from Abundance: Even if your financial resources feel limited, find ways to give from your abundance—your time, attention, skills, or even a smile. Giving from abundance, no matter how small, reinforces your abundant nature and creates energetic space for more abundance to flow to you.

Celebrate Others' Success: Instead of feeling envious when others succeed, celebrate their abundance as proof that prosperity is available to everyone. Their success is evidence that the universe is abundant and that there is plenty for all. Their victory paves the way for your own.

Upgrade Your Language: Notice when you use scarcity language—"I can't afford," "I don't have enough," "I'm broke"—and consciously replace it with abundance language—"I choose to invest my money differently," "I have enough for what matters most," "I am building my wealth."

The Ripple Effect of Abundant Living

When you embody abundance consciousness, it creates waves of prosperity that extend far beyond your personal life. Your family learns that there is enough by watching you live without constant worry about resources. Your children develop healthy relationships with money and abundance because they see you modeling prosperity consciousness. Your friends and colleagues are inspired to examine their own scarcity beliefs when they witness your transformation.

Your abundance also creates practical benefits for your community. When you prosper, you have more resources to share, more capacity to help others, and more energy to contribute to causes you care about. Abundant people create abundant communities, and abundant communities create an abundant world.

This is the beautiful responsibility of abundance consciousness—it is not just about your personal prosperity but about your contribution to collective abundance. When you heal your relationship with money and resources, you help heal the collective scarcity consciousness that creates poverty, inequality, and fear-based economics.

Living from Overflow

I have learned that true abundance consciousness means living from overflow rather than from need. When your cup is full, giving becomes effortless and natural. When you trust in infinite supply, you can be generous without fear. When you know you are always provided for, you can take inspired risks and follow your heart's calling.

Living from overflow does not mean being careless with resources or ignoring practical considerations. It means making decisions from a place of trust rather than fear, opportunity rather than scarcity, expansion rather than contraction. It means asking "How can I create more value?" instead of "How can I get more money?" It means focusing on contribution rather than accumulation.

This shift from scarcity to abundance consciousness changes everything. Work becomes an expression of your gifts rather than just a way to pay bills. Money becomes a tool for good rather than a source of stress. Success becomes about fulfillment rather than just accumulation. Life becomes about thriving rather than just surviving.

The Promise of Prosperity

And so, dear reader, as you complete Days 9-12 of your transformation journey, know that you have laid a powerful foundation of abundance consciousness. You have planted seeds of prosperity that will continue to grow and flourish as you tend them with consistent practice and unwavering faith.

The journey ahead will build upon this foundation of abundance. You will discover your confident nature, your resilient spirit, your magnetic power, your aligned purpose, and your unstoppable force. But all of these discoveries will be enriched by the abundance consciousness you are cultivating now—the deep knowing that you live in a universe of infinite supply and that you are worthy of receiving all the good it has to offer.

Still, you rise, not because you need to acquire more abundance but because you are ready to remember the abundant being you have always been. The light finds you, steady and sure, and in that light, you see the river of abundance that has always been flowing around you, through you, and as you.

Grace finds you here, in this moment of recognition, in this awakening to your abundant nature, in this homecoming to your prosperous self. You are abundant. You have always been abundant. And now, finally, you are ready to live like you believe it.

> *Grace finds us when we finally open our hands and hearts to receive all the good that has been waiting patiently for us to feel worthy of it.*

CHAPTER 4

Daily Transformation - I AM Confident

Days 13-16: Implementing Unshakeable Self-Belief Practices

There is a quiet power that emerges when you finally stop seeking approval from the world and start trusting the wisdom that lives within your own heart. I have stood in that sacred space where self-doubt dissolves and inner knowing rises like the sun at dawn, illuminating everything with clarity and certainty. This is the birthplace of true confidence—not the loud, boastful kind that masks insecurity, but the quiet, unshakeable kind that comes from knowing who you are and whose you are.

Confidence is not something you acquire from external achievements or other people's validation. It is not dependent on your circumstances being perfect or your performance being flawless. True confidence is the natural state of a soul that has remembered its divine nature, that has reconnected with its inherent worth, that has claimed its unlimited potential, and that has aligned with the abundant flow of the universe.

I have learned that confidence is not the absence of fear—it is the presence of faith. It is not about never doubting yourself—it is about trusting yourself even when doubt arises. It is not about being perfect—it is about being perfectly yourself, flaws and all, and knowing that your authentic self is more than enough for whatever life brings your way.

The Nature of True Confidence

For too long, the world has confused confidence with arrogance, self-assurance with self-absorption, inner strength with outer aggression. But I have learned that true confidence is humble, gentle, and quietly powerful. It does not need to prove itself or diminish others to feel strong. It does not require constant external validation or perfect conditions to flourish.

True confidence is rooted in self-acceptance rather than self-perfection. It comes from knowing your worth rather than proving your worth. It emerges from trusting your inner guidance rather than seeking everyone else's approval. It is the natural result of aligning with your authentic self rather than trying to be someone you think you should be.

When you are truly confident, you speak your truth even when your voice shakes. You take action even when you feel uncertain. You show up authentically even when it would be easier to hide. You trust your instincts even when others question your choices. You stand in your power even when the world tries to make you small.

Still, I rise in the knowing that confidence is not a destination but a daily practice. It is not something you achieve once and then possess forever—it is something you choose again and again, moment by moment, day by day. Every time you honor your inner wisdom over external pressure, every time you choose authenticity over approval, every time you trust yourself to handle whatever comes, you are building the unshakeable foundation of true confidence.

Day 13: I AM Confident

Primary Affirmation: "I AM confident in my abilities, my worth, and my capacity to handle whatever life brings."

Supporting Affirmations:

- "I AM worthy of respect and recognition for who I am."

- "I AM capable of learning, growing, and succeeding in all areas of my life."

- "I AM comfortable being authentically myself in any situation."

Morning Ritual: Stand in front of a mirror and look directly into your own eyes. See beyond the surface to the soul within—the eternal, divine, infinitely capable being that you are. Speak your primary affirmation with conviction, allowing your voice to carry the power of your inner truth. Place your hands on your heart and feel the steady rhythm of your confidence. Say aloud: "I trust in my wisdom, I believe in my strength, and I know that I am capable of anything I set my mind to accomplish."

Evening Reflection: Write down three situations from your day where you demonstrated confidence, even in small ways. This might include speaking up in a conversation, making a decision without seeking multiple opinions, or simply walking with your head held high. Celebrate these moments of self-assurance and recognize that confidence is already alive within you—you are simply learning to access it more consistently.

Day 14: I AM Worthy of Success

Primary Affirmation: "I AM worthy of success, recognition, and all the good that comes from living my purpose."

Supporting Affirmations:

- "I AM deserving of opportunities that match my talents and aspirations."

- "I AM confident in my ability to create the success I desire."

- "I AM comfortable receiving praise, recognition, and rewards for my efforts."

Morning Ritual: Write a "Success Resume" that includes not just your professional achievements but all the ways you have succeeded in life—times you overcame challenges, learned from failures, helped others, showed courage, demonstrated kindness, or grew through difficult experiences. Include everything from learning to walk as a child to surviving tough times to mastering skills to creating meaningful relationships. Read this resume aloud and realize that you have a long history of success and capability. End by saying: "I am already successful, and I continue to attract even greater success into my life."

Evening Reflection: Identify one area of your life where you have been hesitant to pursue success because you didn't feel worthy or capable. Write down three reasons why you are absolutely worthy of success in this area, and commit to taking one small step toward this success within the next week.

Day 15: I AM Powerful

Primary Affirmation: "I AM powerful beyond measure, capable of creating positive change in my life and in the world."

Supporting Affirmations:

- "I AM in control of my thoughts, emotions, and responses."

- "I AM able to influence my circumstances through my choices and actions."

- "I AM a force for good in the world, creating ripples of positive impact."

Morning Ritual: Reflect on the different types of power you possess—the power of your words, your choices, your presence, your love, your creativity, your influence, your example. Write down at least ten ways you are powerful, going beyond obvious forms like position or wealth to include subtle but significant forms like the power to make someone smile, to inspire hope, to create beauty, or to bring peace to a situation. Hold this list and feel the truth of your inherent power. Say aloud: "I am powerful not because I control others, but because I have mastered myself. I use my power wisely and lovingly for the highest good of all."

Evening Reflection: Think of one way you used your power positively today—perhaps you chose patience over anger, spoke words of encouragement, made a decision that honored your values, or influenced a situation for the better.

Acknowledge this use of your power and commit to using your power consciously and compassionately tomorrow.

Day 16: I AM Unshakeable

Primary Affirmation: "I AM unshakeable in my faith, my worth, and my commitment to my highest good."

Supporting Affirmations:

- "I AM rooted in my truth and cannot be swayed by external opinions or circumstances."

- "I AM stable, grounded, and secure in who I am."

- "I AM able to remain calm and centered in any storm."

Morning Ritual: Find a tree outside or visualize a strong, ancient tree with deep roots and a sturdy trunk. Place your hands on the tree (or visualize this) and connect with its energy of groundedness and stability. Feel how the tree remains steady through storms, seasons, and years of change. Imagine drawing this same stability into your own being—roots of faith growing deep into the earth, a trunk of self-knowledge growing strong and steady, branches of confidence reaching toward the sky. Say aloud: "Like this tree, I am rooted in truth, grounded in love, and unshakeable in my knowing of who I am."

Evening Reflection: Recall a time when you remained calm and centered during a challenging situation. What inner resources did you draw upon? How did your unshakeable nature serve you and others? Write down the qualities that make you unshakeable and commit to nurturing these qualities even more deeply.

The Psychology of Confidence Building

I have learned that confidence is not just a feeling—it is a skill that can be developed through consistent practice and conscious choice. Psychological research has shown that confidence is built through a combination of self-efficacy (belief in your ability to succeed), self-compassion (treating yourself with kindness), and progressive mastery (gradually taking on bigger challenges).

Your brain is constantly collecting evidence to support or contradict your beliefs about yourself. If you believe you are confident, your brain will notice and remember times when you acted confidently. If you believe you are insecure, your brain will focus on and magnify moments of self-doubt. This is why affirmations are so powerful—they direct your brain to look for evidence of your confidence, creating a positive feedback loop that strengthens your self-belief over time.

Confidence is also closely linked to your self-talk—the internal dialogue that runs through your mind throughout the day. Research has shown that people with high confidence tend to have encouraging, supportive inner voices, while those with low confidence often have critical, judgmental inner voices. By consciously choosing affirming self-talk, you can literally rewire your brain for greater confidence.

The practice of visualization also plays a crucial role in confidence building. When you mentally rehearse success, your brain creates neural pathways as if you had actually experienced that success. This is why athletes visualize their performance before competition—it builds confidence and improves actual performance. By visualizing yourself acting confidently in various situations, you are training your brain for confidence in real life.

The Spiritual Foundation of Confidence

Still, I rise in the understanding that true confidence is not just a psychological state—it is a spiritual recognition of your divine nature. When you truly understand that you are a beloved creation of God, created with infinite love and unique purpose, confidence becomes your natural state. You are not confident because you are better than others—you are confident because you are exactly who you were meant to be.

This spiritual foundation of confidence is unshakeable because it does not depend on external circumstances or achievements. It is not built on what you do but on who you are. It cannot be taken away by failure, criticism, or rejection because it is rooted in your eternal worth and divine connection.

When you pray or meditate, you are connecting with the Source of all confidence—the Divine love that created you and sustains you. In this connection, you remember that you are not alone, that you are guided and supported, that you have access to infinite wisdom and strength. This remembrance naturally breeds confidence because you realize you are part of something much larger and more powerful than yourself.

Your confidence is not separate from your spirituality—it is an expression of your faith, a manifestation of your trust in Divine love, a reflection of your alignment with your highest self. When you are confident, you are not being arrogant—you are being authentic to your spiritual nature.

Overcoming Confidence Blocks

As you journey through Days 13-16, you may encounter internal obstacles that have been undermining your confidence for years. These blocks often stem from past experiences, negative programming, or fear-based beliefs that have convinced you that you are not capable, worthy, or safe to shine your light fully.

Common confidence blocks and their transformations:

Perfectionism: The belief that you must be perfect to be worthy of confidence. *Transformation:* "I am confident in my ability to learn, grow, and improve. My worth is not dependent on my perfection."

Imposter Syndrome: The fear that you are not qualified or that others will discover you don't belong. *Transformation:* "I belong wherever I am, and I bring unique value to every situation. I am constantly learning and growing into my full potential."

Fear of Judgment: The worry about what others will think if you act confidently. *Transformation:* "I cannot control others' opinions, but I can control my own self-respect. I choose to honor my truth regardless of others' reactions."

Past Failures: Using previous mistakes as evidence that you cannot succeed. *Transformation:* "My past failures are my greatest teachers. Each setback has prepared me for greater success and deeper wisdom."

Comparison: Measuring your confidence against others' achievements or abilities. *Transformation:* "I am on my own unique path. My confidence comes from my authentic self, not from being better than others."

When these blocks arise, meet them with compassion rather than resistance. They are not your enemies—they are old protections that once served a purpose but are now holding you back. Thank them for their service, then gently replace them with confidence-building truths.

The Energy of Confidence

I have learned that confidence has a distinct energetic signature that you can feel in your body and that others can sense in your presence. Confident energy is expansive, open, and grounded. It creates a sense of ease in your body— shoulders back, chest open, head held high, breathing deep and natural. It radiates from your core and fills the space around you with calm strength.

When you are in confident energy, you naturally attract opportunities, respect, and positive interactions. People are drawn to confident energy because it feels safe, inspiring, and empowering. Your confidence gives others permission to be confident too, creating a positive ripple effect in all your relationships and interactions.

Learning to recognize and cultivate confident energy is as important as the thoughts and beliefs of confidence. Practice carrying yourself with confidence even when you don't feel it internally. Stand tall, make eye contact, speak clearly, and move with purpose. This physical practice of confidence sends signals to your brain that you are confident, which in turn creates the internal experience of confidence.

Your voice is also a powerful tool for confidence building. Practice speaking with clarity, conviction, and appropriate volume. Avoid uptalk (ending statements with a questioning tone) and filler words that undermine your message. Let your voice carry the authority of your inner truth.

Confidence in Action

Beyond your daily affirmations and rituals, there are specific actions you can take to build and demonstrate confidence in your daily life:

Set and Keep Commitments to Yourself: Every time you make a promise to yourself and keep it, you build self-trust and confidence. Start with small commitments—like drinking more water or reading for ten minutes—and gradually work up to bigger ones.

Speak Up in Meetings or Groups: Practice sharing your ideas, asking questions, and contributing to conversations. Each time you speak up, you build confidence in your voice and your worth.

Take on New Challenges: Gradually stretch beyond your comfort zone by taking on tasks or opportunities that require you to grow. Success builds confidence, but so does the simple act of trying.

Dress for Confidence: Wear clothes that make you feel good about yourself. When you look good, you feel good, and when you feel good, you act with more confidence.

Practice Good Posture: Stand and sit with your shoulders back, head high, and spine straight. Your posture communicates confidence to others and signals confidence to your own brain.

Learn Something New: Confidence grows when you prove to yourself that you can learn and master new skills. Take a class, read a book, or practice a new hobby.

The Ripple Effect of Confidence

When you embody true confidence, it creates waves of positive impact that extend far beyond your personal life. Your children learn self assurance by watching you model confidence. Your friends and colleagues are inspired to be more confident themselves when they see you standing in your power. Your community benefits from your contributions when you are confident enough to share your gifts fully.

Confident people create confident communities, and confident communities create positive change in the world. When you are confident, you are more likely to take risks, pursue your dreams, stand up for what is right, and contribute your unique talents to the world. Your confidence is not just for you—it is for everyone whose life you touch.

This is the beautiful responsibility of confidence—it is not about being better than others but about being your best self so that you can inspire others to be their best selves too. When you shine your light fully, you give others permission to shine theirs.

Living Confidently

I have learned that living confidently is not about never feeling doubt or fear—it is about feeling those emotions and choosing to act from your deeper truth anyway. It is about trusting yourself to handle whatever comes, even when you don't know exactly how. It is about believing in your ability to figure things out, learn from mistakes, and grow through challenges.

Confident living means making decisions from your inner wisdom rather than external pressure. It means saying yes to opportunities that align with your values and no to those that do not. It means expressing your authentic self even when it would be easier to conform. It means taking up space, speaking your truth, and honoring your worth in every interaction.

This does not mean being aggressive, domineering, or insensitive to others. True confidence is gentle strength—powerful but not pushy, sure but not arrogant, assertive but not aggressive. It honors both your own worth and the worth of others.

The Unshakeable Foundation

And so, dear reader, as you complete Days 13-16 of your transformation journey, know that you have built an unshakeable foundation of confidence. You have remembered your inherent worth, claimed your unlimited potential, aligned with abundant flow, and now you are standing in your power with quiet certainty and grace.

The journey ahead will build upon this foundation of confidence. You will discover your resilient nature, your magnetic power, your aligned purpose, and your unstoppable force. But all of these discoveries will be strengthened by the confidence you are cultivating now—the deep knowing that you are capable, worthy, and powerful beyond measure.

Still, you rise, not because you need to prove your confidence to anyone, but because you are ready to live from the truth of your confident nature. The light finds you, steady and sure, and in that light, you see the powerful, capable, magnificent being you have always been.

Grace finds you here, in this moment of recognition, in this claiming of your power, in this homecoming to your confident self. You are confident. You have always been confident. And now, finally, you are ready to live like you believe it.

Grace finds us when we finally have the courage to trust ourselves as deeply as God trusts us.

CHAPTER 5

Overcoming Obstacles - I AM Resilient

Days 17-20: Handling Setbacks with Grace and Strength

There is a sacred space between the breaking and the breaking open, between the storm and the calm that follows, between the end of what was and the beginning of what will be. I have stood in that space, heart shattered but spirit unbroken, and I have learned that resilience is not about avoiding the storms of life—it is about learning to dance in the rain, to find your footing on shifting ground, to discover that you are stronger than anything that tries to break you.

Resilience is not the absence of pain—it is the presence of an unshakeable faith that carries you through the pain. It is not about being invulnerable—it is about being vulnerable and rising anyway. It is not about never falling—it is about falling and getting back up, again and again, until standing becomes your natural state not because you have never been knocked down, but because you have learned the sacred art of rising.

I have learned that resilience is not something you are born with or without—it is something you build, one choice at a time, one breath at a time, one day at a time. Every time you choose hope over despair, courage over fear, faith over doubt, you are strengthening the spiritual muscle of resilience. Every time you get back up after being knocked down, you are proving to yourself and the universe that you are indeed unbreakable in your essence, even when your circumstances feel overwhelming.

The Nature of True Resilience

For too long, the world has taught us that resilience means suffering in silence, that strength means hiding our struggles, that courage means pretending we are not afraid. But I have learned that true resilience is not about pretending to be invincible—it is about being honest about your vulnerabilities while refusing to let them define your destiny.

True resilience is tender strength—it acknowledges the pain while refusing to be consumed by it. It honors the tears while insisting on the sunrise. It validates the struggle while maintaining faith in the breakthrough. It says, "Yes, this hurts, and yes, I will survive it. Yes, this is difficult, and yes, I will find a way through. Yes, this has broken me, and yes, I will heal stronger than before."

When you are truly resilient, you understand that every setback is a setup for a comeback, that every breakdown is a breakthrough in disguise, that every ending is a new beginning waiting to unfold. You know that the same force that allows a seed to break through concrete, that enables a butterfly to emerge from a cocoon, that causes the sun to rise after every night, is the same force that lives within you, ready to lift you up no matter how many times life knocks you down.

Still, I rise in the knowing that resilience is not about being hard or cold or disconnected from your feelings. It is about being soft enough to feel everything deeply while being strong enough to not let those feelings destroy you. It is about having a heart that can break and heal, break and heal, expanding with each cycle into greater capacity for love, compassion, and joy.

Day 17: I AM Resilient

Primary Affirmation: "I AM resilient, capable of bouncing back from any setback with grace and strength."

Supporting Affirmations:

- "I AM stronger than any challenge I face."

- "I AM able to find meaning and growth in every experience."

- "I AM protected and guided through all of life's difficulties."

Morning Ritual: Think of a tree that has weathered many storms—its branches may be scarred, some may have broken, but its roots have grown deeper, its trunk has grown stronger, and it continues to reach toward the light. Visualize yourself as this tree, recognizing that every storm you have survived has made you more resilient. Place your hands over your heart and feel the steady beat of your survival, the rhythm of your resilience. Say aloud: "I have survived 100% of my difficult days so far. I am resilient, I am strong, and I am capable of weathering any storm that comes my way."

Evening Reflection: Write about a time when you demonstrated resilience—when you faced a challenge, setback, or loss and found a way to keep going. What inner resources did you draw upon? What lessons did you learn? How did this experience make you stronger? Celebrate your resilience and acknowledge that this strength is always available to you.

Day 18: I AM Unbreakable

Primary Affirmation: "I AM unbreakable in my spirit, no matter what challenges come my way."

Supporting Affirmations:

- "I AM flexible enough to bend without breaking."

- "I AM rooted in my faith and cannot be shaken at my core."

- "I AM able to transform any obstacle into an opportunity."

Morning Ritual: Hold a piece of bamboo or visualize bamboo swaying in the wind. Notice how it bends dramatically but never breaks, how it yields to the force but springs back to its original position. This is the nature of your unbreakable spirit—not rigid and brittle, but flexible and resilient. Connect with this energy of flexibility within yourself. Say aloud: "Like bamboo, I am strong enough to endure and flexible enough to adapt. I bend but do not break. I yield but do not surrender. My spirit is unbreakable."

Evening Reflection: Identify one area of your life where you have been too rigid or inflexible. How might approaching this situation with bamboo-like flexibility serve you better? Write down one way you can practice being more adaptable in this area while maintaining your core strength and values.

Day 19: I AM Victorious

Primary Affirmation: "I AM victorious over every challenge, transforming obstacles into stepping stones."

Supporting Affirmations:

- "I AM destined to overcome and achieve my dreams."

- "I AM learning and growing stronger from every experience."

- "I AM more than a conqueror through the strength that lives within me."

Morning Ritual: Create a "Victory List" of all the challenges you have overcome in your life—include big and small victories, from learning to ride a bike to surviving loss, from overcoming fears to achieving goals. Read this list aloud and feel the power of your proven track record of victory. Realize that you are not just a survivor—you are a thriver, a victor, a champion of your own life. Say aloud: "I am victorious. Every challenge I have faced has made me stronger, wiser, and more capable. I face today's challenges with the confidence of someone who has already won."

Evening Reflection: Think of a current challenge or obstacle in your life. Instead of focusing on how difficult it is, write about how overcoming this challenge will make you stronger, what you will learn from it, and how it might be preparing you for something better. Shift your perspective from victim to victor.

Day 20: I AM Healing

Primary Affirmation: "I AM healing, growing, and becoming whole through every experience."

Supporting Affirmations:

- "I AM releasing what no longer serves me and embracing what helps me grow."

- "I AM patient and gentle with myself as I heal and transform."

- "I AM grateful for my journey, including the painful parts that have taught me resilience."

Morning Ritual: Place your hands over any part of your body that feels tense, hurt, or in need of healing—this could be your heart, your head, your shoulders, or anywhere else. Send love and healing energy to this part of yourself. Visualize golden light flowing from your hands into the area that needs healing. Say aloud: "I am healing on all levels—physically, emotionally, mentally, and spiritually. Every cell in my body is regenerating with perfect health. Every wound in my heart is healing with perfect love. I am becoming whole."

Evening Reflection: Write a letter of forgiveness to yourself for any ways you feel you have fallen short, made mistakes, or not lived up to your own expectations. Include forgiveness for any self-judgment, criticism, or harsh treatment you have given yourself. End the letter with a commitment to treat yourself with the same compassion you would show a beloved friend who was healing from pain.

The Science of Resilience

I have learned that resilience is not just a spiritual quality—it is a measurable capacity that can be developed through specific practices and mindset shifts. Neuroscience has shown us that resilient people have certain brain patterns and neural pathways that can be cultivated through intentional practice.

Resilient individuals tend to have stronger prefrontal cortex activity, which is responsible for executive function, emotional regulation, and perspective-taking. They also show greater neuroplasticity—the brain's ability to form new neural connections—which allows them to adapt more readily to changing circumstances and recover more quickly from setbacks.

One of the key factors in building resilience is what psychologists call "cognitive flexibility"—the ability to shift your thinking patterns and see situations from multiple perspectives. When you practice affirmations like "I AM resilient" and "I AM unbreakable," you are literally training your brain to default to resilient thinking patterns rather than victim mentality.

Research has also shown that resilient people tend to have what's called an "internal locus of control"—they believe they have the power to influence their circumstances rather than being at the mercy of external forces. While they acknowledge that they cannot control everything that happens to them, they focus on what they can control: their thoughts, their responses, their actions, and their attitudes.

The practice of gratitude, which is woven throughout this resilience work, has been scientifically proven to increase resilience by rewiring the brain to notice positive aspects of experiences, even difficult ones. When you consistently look for lessons, growth, and meaning in your challenges, you train your brain to see setbacks as temporary and surmountable rather than permanent and devastating.

The Spiritual Dimension of Resilience

Still, I rise in the understanding that resilience is ultimately a spiritual practice—a deep trust in the benevolent nature of the universe and your place within it. When you truly believe that you are loved, guided, and supported by a higher power, resilience becomes your natural response to adversity rather than a skill you must force yourself to develop.

This spiritual foundation of resilience is what allows you to maintain hope in the darkest times, to find meaning in the most difficult experiences, and to trust that everything is working together for your highest good, even when you cannot see the bigger picture. It is what enables you to surrender control while maintaining faith, to be vulnerable while remaining strong, to accept what is while continuing to work toward what could be.

Prayer and meditation are powerful tools for building resilience because they connect you to a source of strength that is larger than your circumstances. When you take time to be still and connect with the Divine, you remember that you are not alone in your struggles, that you have access to infinite wisdom and strength, and that your current challenges are temporary while your spiritual nature is eternal.

Your resilience is not separate from your spirituality—it is an expression of your faith, a manifestation of your trust in Divine love, a reflection of your knowing that you are held and carried through every storm. When you are resilient, you are not just being strong—you are being faithful to your divine nature.

The Alchemy of Transformation

I have learned that true resilience involves a kind of spiritual alchemy—the ability to transform pain into purpose, wounds into wisdom, setbacks into strength. This is not about pretending that difficult experiences are good or denying the reality of pain—it is about finding the gold hidden within the darkness, the gifts wrapped in the challenges, the blessings disguised as burdens.

Every obstacle you face carries within it the seeds of your next level of growth. Every setback contains the wisdom you need for your next breakthrough. Every wound becomes a place where light can enter, where compassion can grow, where strength can be born. This is the sacred work of resilience—not just surviving your difficulties but allowing them to transform you into someone stronger, wiser, and more loving.

This alchemical process requires patience, faith, and a willingness to see beyond the immediate pain to the ultimate purpose. It requires trusting that your struggles are not meaningless but meaningful, not random but purposeful, not punishment but preparation for something greater.

When you embrace this perspective, you begin to see your challenges differently. Instead of asking "Why is this happening to me?" you begin to ask "What is this teaching me?" Instead of feeling victimized by your circumstances, you begin to feel empowered by your ability to transform them. Instead of seeing yourself as broken by your experiences, you begin to see yourself as being broken open to greater capacity for love, joy, and service.

Common Resilience Challenges

As you journey through Days 17-20, you may encounter specific challenges that test your resilience. I want to prepare you for these common obstacles so that you can move through them with greater ease and grace:

The Comparison Trap: Comparing your struggles to others' successes or your healing timeline to someone else's recovery. Remember that everyone's journey is unique, and resilience is not about being stronger than others—it's about being true to your own path.

The Perfectionism Prison: Expecting yourself to be resilient all the time, to never feel overwhelmed or discouraged. True resilience includes the permission to have difficult days while maintaining faith that better days are coming.

The Victim Mentality: Getting stuck in the story of how unfair life has been to you. While it's important to acknowledge injustices and validate your pain, resilience requires eventually shifting from "Why me?" to "What now?"

The Independence Illusion: Believing that resilience means handling everything alone. True resilience often involves knowing when to ask for help, when to lean on others, and when to accept support.

The Impatience Trap: Expecting healing and growth to happen on your timeline. Resilience requires accepting that transformation is a process that cannot be rushed but must be trusted.

When these challenges arise, meet them with the same compassion you would show a dear friend who was struggling. Remember that developing resilience is itself a practice in resilience—it requires patience, self-compassion, and the willingness to begin again when you stumble.

Building Your Resilience Toolkit

Beyond your daily affirmations and rituals, there are specific practices and tools that can strengthen your resilience over time:

Develop a Support Network: Cultivate relationships with people who believe in your strength and can offer encouragement during difficult times. Resilience is often a team sport, not a solo endeavor.

Practice Mindfulness: Learn to observe your thoughts and emotions without being overwhelmed by them. Mindfulness helps you respond to challenges rather than react to them.

Create Meaning from Adversity: Look for lessons, growth opportunities, and ways your difficult experiences can help others. When you find meaning in your pain, it becomes more bearable and transformative.

Maintain Healthy Habits: Regular exercise, adequate sleep, nutritious eating, and stress management practices provide the physical foundation for emotional and mental resilience.

Develop Problem-Solving Skills: Practice breaking down challenges into manageable steps. When you know you can figure things out, you approach difficulties with confidence rather than panic.

Cultivate Optimism: While acknowledging realistic challenges, practice focusing on possibilities, solutions, and positive outcomes. Optimism is a learnable skill that greatly enhances resilience.

Keep a Gratitude Practice: Regularly acknowledging what you're grateful for, even during difficult times, helps maintain perspective and hope.

The Ripple Effect of Resilience

When you embody true resilience, it creates waves of strength and hope that extend far beyond your personal life. Your children learn that challenges are temporary and surmountable when they see you weather storms with grace. Your friends and colleagues are inspired to persevere through their own difficulties when they witness your resilience. Your community benefits from your example of how to transform pain into purpose.

Resilient people create resilient communities, and resilient communities create positive change in the world. When you are resilient, you are more likely to take risks, pursue meaningful goals, help others through their struggles, and contribute to solutions rather than getting stuck in problems.

This is the beautiful responsibility of resilience—it is not just about your personal strength but about the strength you bring to the collective human experience. Your resilience gives others permission to be resilient too, creating a ripple effect of hope and healing that extends far beyond what you can see.

Living Resiliently

I have learned that living resiliently is not about never falling down—it is about getting up every time you fall, about finding the lesson in every loss, about maintaining faith in the face of uncertainty. It is about approaching each new challenge with the confidence that comes from having survived previous ones, the wisdom that comes from having learned from your experiences, and the strength that comes from knowing you are never alone.

Resilient living means making peace with the fact that life includes both joy and sorrow, success and failure, ease and difficulty. It means embracing the full spectrum of human experience while refusing to let any single experience define your entire story. It means knowing that you are not just surviving your life—you are actively creating it, one resilient choice at a time.

This does not mean being passive or accepting harmful situations. True resilience often requires courageous action—setting boundaries, making difficult changes, standing up for yourself and others. But it does mean approaching these challenges from a place of strength rather than weakness, faith rather than fear, hope rather than despair.

The Unbreakable Spirit

And so, dear reader, as you complete Days 17-20 of your transformation journey, know that you have awakened to the unbreakable nature of your spirit. You have remembered that you are made of stardust and steel, of tenderness and strength, of vulnerability and power. You have claimed your resilience as your birthright and your superpower.

The journey ahead will continue to build upon this foundation of resilience. You will discover your magnetic nature, your aligned purpose, and your unstoppable force. But all of these discoveries will be strengthened by the resilience you are cultivating now—the deep knowing that you can handle anything life brings because you have already handled so much with such grace.

Still, you rise, not because you have to prove your strength to anyone, but because rising is your nature, resilience is your essence, and victory is your destiny. The light finds you, steady and sure, and in that light, you see the warrior, the survivor, the thriver you have always been.

Grace finds you here, in this moment of recognition, in this claiming of your resilience, in this homecoming to your unbreakable self. You are resilient. You have always been resilient. And now, finally, you are ready to live like you believe it.

Grace finds us when we finally understand that our scars are not signs of weakness but evidence of our strength, not marks of failure but medals of survival.

CHAPTER 6

Deepening Practice - I AM Magnetic

Days 21-24: Advanced Techniques for Attracting Your Desires

There is a secret force that flows through all of creation, invisible yet undeniable, drawing like to like, aligning energy with its match, orchestrating the dance of attraction that governs everything from the orbit of planets to the beating of hearts. I have felt this force moving through my life, pulling toward me the people, opportunities, and experiences that resonate with my deepest truth, and I have learned that this magnetic power is not reserved for the lucky few—it lives within every soul, waiting to be awakened, acknowledged, and aligned with conscious intention.

You are magnetic. Not in some mystical, unattainable way, but in the most practical, scientific sense. Every thought you think, every emotion you feel, every belief you hold creates an energetic signature that attracts matching experiences into your life. You are constantly broadcasting a signal to the universe, and the universe is constantly responding by bringing you more of whatever you are predominantly focused on, feeling, and believing.

I have learned that magnetism is not about manipulation or forcing outcomes—it is about alignment, about becoming so clear about who you are and what you want that the universe cannot help but deliver experiences that match your energetic frequency. It is about raising your vibration to such a level of love, joy, gratitude, and authenticity that everything good in the universe is naturally drawn to you like iron filings to a magnet.

The Nature of Magnetic Attraction

For too long, we have believed that getting what we want requires struggle, force, and endless effort. We have been taught that good things come to those who fight for them, that success requires sacrifice, that love must be earned through pleasing others. But I have learned that this pushing, striving, forcing energy actually repels what we desire most, while the energy of magnetic attraction draws it to us with grace and ease.

True magnetism is not about being perfect or having everything figured out—it is about being authentic, aligned, and appreciative. It is about knowing your worth so deeply that you naturally attract people and experiences that honor that worth. It is about being so genuinely happy and grateful for what you have that the universe wants to give you more to be happy and grateful about.

When you are truly magnetic, you do not chase opportunities—opportunities chase you. You do not beg for love—love finds you irresistible. You do not struggle for success—success flows to you naturally. You do not worry about lack—abundance seeks you out. This is not about being entitled or passive, but about being so aligned with your authentic self and your highest good that the universe conspires to support your dreams.

Still, I rise in the knowing that magnetism is not a destination but a way of being. It is not something you achieve once and then possess forever—it is something you cultivate daily through your thoughts, feelings, actions, and intentions. Every moment offers you the choice to align with magnetic energy or to resist it, to attract what you want or to repel it through fear, doubt, or misalignment.

Day 21: I AM Magnetic

Primary Affirmation: "I AM magnetic, naturally attracting everything that aligns with my highest good."

Supporting Affirmations:

- "I AM a powerful magnet for love, abundance, and opportunity."

- "I AM aligned with my authentic self and attract authentic experiences."

- "I AM irresistibly attractive to all that is meant for me."

Morning Ritual: Stand in front of a mirror and imagine yourself surrounded by a brilliant golden light—this is your magnetic field, your energetic signature that attracts matching experiences. See this light growing brighter and stronger as you speak your affirmations. Visualize this magnetic energy drawing to you everything you desire— loving relationships, abundant opportunities, perfect health, creative inspiration, financial prosperity. Feel yourself becoming more magnetic with each breath. Say aloud: "I am a magnet for miracles. I attract with ease what others struggle to find. My authentic self is irresistible to my highest good."

Evening Reflection: Write down three things that were attracted into your life today—this could be a kind word from a stranger, an unexpected opportunity, a solution to a problem, or simply feeling good about yourself. Recognize that these attractions, no matter how small, are evidence of your magnetic power. Celebrate your ability to attract positive experiences.

Day 22: I AM Irresistible

Primary Affirmation: "I AM irresistible to my dreams, my soulmate, and my destiny."

Supporting Affirmations:

- "I AM so aligned with my truth that my desires cannot resist me."

- "I AM magnetically attractive to people who appreciate my authentic self."

- "I AM irresistibly drawn to opportunities that serve my highest purpose."

Morning Ritual: Write a love letter to yourself describing all the qualities that make you irresistible—your kindness, your creativity, your sense of humor, your resilience, your passion, your unique perspective, your capacity for love. Include not just your best qualities but also your quirks, your imperfections, and your authentic humanity. Read this letter aloud with conviction, allowing yourself to feel genuinely attractive and lovable. Say aloud: "I am irresistible because I am authentically me. There is no one else like me in the universe, and that makes me invaluable."

Evening Reflection: Think of someone you find irresistibly attractive—not just physically, but energetically. What is it about their energy that draws you to them? How can you cultivate more of these same qualities in yourself? Write down three ways you can become more irresistibly yourself.

Day 23: I AM Aligned

Primary Affirmation: "I AM perfectly aligned with my desires, and they flow to me with divine timing."

Supporting Affirmations:

- "I AM in harmony with the universe and trust its perfect timing."

- "I AM aligned with my purpose and attract opportunities that serve it."

- "I AM synchronized with the flow of universal abundance."

Morning Ritual: Sit quietly and imagine yourself as a tuning fork that has been struck and is now vibrating at the perfect frequency. Feel this vibration of alignment resonating through every cell of your body. Imagine that this vibration is sending out a signal to the universe, calling to you everything that matches this frequency of alignment. Visualize your desires responding to this call, moving toward you like music drawn to a musician, like bees drawn to nectar. Say aloud: "I am perfectly aligned with my highest good. My desires and I are vibrating at the same frequency, and we are drawing each other together."

Evening Reflection: Reflect on moments during the day when you felt most aligned—times when you were in flow, when things felt easy and natural, when you felt connected to your purpose. What were you doing? How were you feeling? How can you create more of these aligned moments in your life?

Day 24: I AM Receptive

Primary Affirmation: "I AM open and receptive to receiving all the good the universe wants to give me."

Supporting Affirmations:

- "I AM worthy of receiving abundance from expected and unexpected sources."

- "I AM grateful for what I have and excited about what is coming."

- "I AM ready to receive blessings that exceed my wildest dreams."

Morning Ritual: Practice the physical gesture of receiving by standing with your arms open wide, palms facing up, as if you are ready to catch falling blessings from the sky. Feel the energy of receptivity in your body—open, welcoming, ready to receive. Breathe deeply and imagine golden light flowing into your open palms, filling your heart, and radiating throughout your entire being. Say aloud: "I am open to receive. I am ready to receive. I am grateful to receive. I welcome all good into my life with open arms and an open heart."

Evening Reflection: Write down all the ways you received today—love, kindness, opportunities, information, help, beauty, joy. Include both the obvious gifts and the subtle ones you might have overlooked. Notice how much you are already receiving, and express gratitude for your ability to attract and accept good into your life.

The Science of Magnetic Attraction

I have learned that magnetism is not just a metaphor—it is a scientifically measurable phenomenon. Every thought you think creates electrical activity in your brain, and this electrical activity creates a magnetic field around your head. Your heart, which generates an electromagnetic field 60 times stronger than your brain, broadcasts your emotional state far beyond your physical body. You are literally a walking, talking electromagnetic being, constantly emitting signals that influence your environment and attract matching experiences.

Quantum physics has shown us that at the subatomic level, everything is energy vibrating at different frequencies. The law of attraction, which governs magnetic attraction, is simply the principle that like frequencies attract like frequencies. When you consistently think thoughts of abundance, feel emotions of gratitude, and take actions aligned with your desires, you create a coherent energetic signal that the universe responds to by bringing you more experiences that match this signal.

Neuroscience has revealed that your brain has a built-in filtering system called the reticular activating system (RAS) that determines what information you notice and what you ignore. When you focus on what you want with emotion and intention, your RAS begins to filter your perceptions to show you opportunities, resources, and possibilities that were always there but previously invisible to you. This is why when you decide to buy a red car, you suddenly see red cars everywhere—they were always there, but now your brain is programmed to notice them.

The practice of visualization, which is central to magnetic attraction, has been shown to create the same neural pathways as actually experiencing what you're visualizing. When you regularly visualize yourself having what you desire, feeling how it feels to have it, and expressing gratitude for receiving it, you are literally programming your brain to recognize and attract these experiences when they appear in your life.

The Spiritual Dimension of Magnetism

Still, I rise in the understanding that true magnetism is not just about attracting external things—it is about aligning with your divine nature and allowing God's love to flow through you so powerfully that it naturally draws to you everything that serves your highest good and the good of all.

When you are truly magnetic, you are not manipulating or forcing outcomes—you are surrendering to the perfect intelligence of divine love and trusting that what is meant for you will find you. You are not trying to bend the universe to your will—you are aligning your will with the universe's desire to bless you abundantly. You are not seeking to get what you want through clever techniques—you are becoming the kind of person who naturally attracts what they need through their authentic presence and aligned action.

This spiritual dimension of magnetism requires a deep trust in the benevolent nature of the universe and your place within it. It requires believing that you are not separate from the creative force of life but an integral part of it, and that this force wants you to thrive, to be happy, to fulfill your purpose, and to experience the fullness of love and abundance.

Prayer and meditation are powerful tools for developing magnetic attraction because they align you with divine will and open you to receive divine guidance. When you take time to connect with your Creator, you remember that you are not alone in your desires, that you have access to infinite intelligence and resources, and that your dreams are not just personal fantasies but divine impulses meant to be fulfilled.

The Energy of Attraction vs. Repulsion

I have learned that understanding the difference between attractive and repulsive energy is crucial to developing your magnetic power. Attractive energy is characterized by love, gratitude, joy, confidence, trust, and alignment. It feels expansive, open, and flowing. When you are in attractive energy, you naturally draw positive experiences to you because your energetic signature is one of receptivity and appreciation.

Repulsive energy is characterized by fear, lack, desperation, neediness, control, and resistance. It feels contracted, closed, and stuck. When you are in repulsive energy, you actually push away what you desire most because your energetic signature is one of scarcity and separation.

The key to magnetic attraction is learning to recognize when you are in repulsive energy and consciously shifting back to attractive energy. This is not about suppressing negative emotions or pretending to feel good when you don't—it is about acknowledging your feelings with compassion and then choosing thoughts and actions that align you with what you want to attract.

When you notice yourself feeling desperate about finding love, shift to feeling grateful for the love you already have in your life. When you catch yourself worrying about money, shift to appreciating the abundance you currently enjoy. When you find yourself frustrated that your dreams haven't manifested yet, shift to excitement about the perfect timing of their arrival.

Advanced Magnetic Techniques

As you deepen your practice of magnetic attraction, there are advanced techniques that can amplify your power to draw your desires to you:

Emotional Embodiment: Don't just visualize having what you want—feel what it would feel like to have it. Emotion is the fuel of attraction. Spend time each day feeling genuinely grateful for your desires as if they have already manifested. This creates a magnetic pull that draws them into your reality.

Future Self Visualization: Regularly visualize yourself as the person who has already achieved your dreams. How do you walk, talk, dress, think, and feel? Embody this future self in your daily life, making decisions from this elevated identity rather than your current circumstances.

Magnetic Journaling: Write in your journal as if your desires have already manifested. "I am so grateful that..." "I love how it feels to..." "I am amazed by how easily..." This technique programs your subconscious mind to accept your desires as reality.

Energy Clearing: Regularly clear limiting beliefs, negative emotions, and resistant thoughts that block your magnetic field. Use techniques like meditation, energy healing, or simply asking for divine assistance in releasing what no longer serves you.

Alignment Actions: Take actions that demonstrate your faith in your desires manifesting. If you want a new job, update your resume and start networking. If you want love, make space in your life and your heart for a partner. These actions signal to the universe that you are serious about your desires.

Gratitude Amplification: The more genuinely grateful you are for what you have, the more magnetic you become for receiving more. Make gratitude a daily practice, finding reasons to appreciate your life even in its current form.

Common Attraction Blocks

As you develop your magnetic power, you may encounter internal blocks that interfere with your ability to attract what you desire. These blocks often stem from deep-seated beliefs about your worthiness, safety, or the nature of the universe itself:

Worthiness Issues: Believing deep down that you don't deserve what you want. Antidote: Daily affirmations of your inherent worth and divine right to happiness and abundance.

Safety Concerns: Unconscious fear that having what you want will somehow be dangerous or create problems. Antidote: Visualizing yourself safely enjoying your desires and seeing how they enhance rather than threaten your life.

Attachment to Outcomes: Gripping so tightly to specific outcomes that you block the universe from delivering something even better. Antidote: Holding your desires lightly, trusting that what comes will be perfect for you.

Lack of Faith: Doubting that the universe is truly abundant and benevolent. Antidote: Collecting evidence of divine generosity in your life and others' lives, building a foundation of trust in universal love.

Mixed Messages: Saying you want something while unconsciously believing or acting as if you don't. Antidote: Becoming aware of your conflicting beliefs and aligning all parts of yourself with your desires.

The Magnetism of Authenticity

I have learned that the most powerful form of magnetism comes not from trying to be attractive to others but from being authentically yourself. When you stop trying to be what you think others want and start being who you truly are, you naturally attract people and experiences that appreciate and support your authentic self.

This authentic magnetism is not about being perfect—it is about being real. It is not about having everything figured out—it is about being honest about your journey. It is not about never feeling doubt or fear—it is about feeling these emotions and choosing to move forward anyway.

When you are authentically magnetic, you do not try to be everything to everyone—you are fully yourself and trust that this is enough. You do not hide your flaws or weaknesses—you embrace them as part of your human experience. You do not pretend to be further along than you are—you meet yourself and others exactly where you are with compassion and honesty.

This authenticity creates a powerful magnetic field because it is rare and refreshing in a world full of pretense and performance. People are drawn to authenticity because it gives them permission to be authentic too. Opportunities are attracted to authenticity because it creates trust and genuine connection.

The Ripple Effect of Magnetic Living

When you embody magnetic attraction, it creates waves of positive energy that extend far beyond your personal life. Your friends and family are inspired to raise their own vibration when they see you living in alignment with your desires. Your community benefits from the positive energy you bring to every interaction. Your example shows others that it is possible to attract what you want through love rather than struggle.

Magnetic people create magnetic environments wherever they go. They uplift others, inspire hope, and demonstrate that life can be joyful, abundant, and fulfilling. Their very presence raises the vibration of any space they enter, making it easier for everyone around them to attract positive experiences.

This is the beautiful responsibility of magnetic living—it is not just about attracting what you want but about becoming the kind of person who helps others attract what they want too. Your magnetism is not meant to be hoarded but shared, not meant to separate you from others but to connect you more deeply with all of life.

Living Magnetically

I have learned that living magnetically is not about constantly focusing on what you want to attract—it is about becoming the kind of person who naturally attracts good things because of who you are being, not what you are doing. It is about cultivating an energy of love, joy, gratitude, and trust that makes you irresistible to your highest good.

Magnetic living means waking up each day in appreciation for what you have while remaining open to receiving more. It means making decisions from love rather than fear, from abundance rather than scarcity, from trust rather than control. It means following your joy, honoring your intuition, and taking inspired action when it feels right.

This does not mean being passive or waiting for things to happen to you. Magnetic living often requires courage, action, and willingness to step outside your comfort zone. But it means taking these actions from a place of alignment and enthusiasm rather than desperation and struggle.

The Magnetic Future

And so, dear reader, as you complete Days 21-24 of your transformation journey, know that you have activated one of the most powerful forces in the universe—your magnetic attraction. You have remembered that you are not a victim of circumstance but a creator of experience, not at the mercy of chance but in partnership with divine intelligence.

The journey ahead will continue to build upon this foundation of magnetic attraction. You will discover your aligned purpose and your unstoppable force. But all of these discoveries will be enhanced by the magnetism you are cultivating now—the deep knowing that you are a powerful attractor of everything that serves your highest good and the good of all.

Still, you rise, not because you need to force or chase what you want, but because you are ready to become so magnetic that what you want cannot help but find you. The light finds you, steady and sure, and in that light, you see the irresistible, magnetic, powerfully attractive being you have always been.

Grace finds you here, in this moment of recognition, in this claiming of your magnetic power, in this homecoming to your attractive self. You are magnetic. You have always been magnetic. And now, finally, you are ready to live like you believe it.

Grace finds us when we finally understand that we are not here to chase our dreams but to become so aligned with our truth that our dreams chase us.

CHAPTER 7

Living Your Truth -
I AM Aligned

*Days 25-28: Integration with Your
Authentic Self and Purpose*

There comes a moment in every soul's journey when the scattered pieces of who you have been, who you are, and who you are becoming suddenly arrange themselves into a beautiful, coherent whole. I have stood at that sacred intersection where purpose meets passion, where calling meets courage, where the deepest truth of your being aligns perfectly with the highest expression of your life, and I have learned that this alignment is not a destination you reach but a way of being you choose, again and again, in each precious moment you are given.

Alignment is the harmony between your inner world and your outer world, between your values and your actions, between your dreams and your daily choices. It is the sweet resonance that occurs when every part of your life sings the same song, when your work feels like worship, when your relationships reflect your worth, when your choices honor your deepest knowing, and when your very existence becomes a prayer of authenticity offered to the world.

I have learned that living in alignment is not about perfection—it is about integration. It is not about having everything figured out—it is about trusting the wisdom that lives within you. It is not about eliminating all conflicts and challenges—it is about navigating them from your center, from your truth, from the unshakeable knowing of who you are and whose you are.

The Nature of True Alignment

For too long, we have been taught to fragment ourselves—to be one person at work and another at home, to hide our spiritual nature in professional settings, to suppress our authentic desires in favor of others' expectations. We have learned to compartmentalize our lives, to wear different masks for different occasions, to split ourselves into acceptable and unacceptable parts. But I have learned that this fragmentation is the source of our deepest suffering and the greatest barrier to our joy.

True alignment is about wholeness, about bringing all parts of yourself into harmony, about living as an integrated being who honors every aspect of your nature. It is about being the same authentic self in every context, allowing your values to guide your decisions, and expressing your unique gifts in whatever you do.

When you are truly aligned, there is no war within you between what you want and what you think you should want, between who you are and who you think you should be, between what brings you joy and what brings you approval. You move through life with a sense of integrity and purpose that comes from knowing you are living in accordance with your deepest truth.

Still, I rise in the knowing that alignment is not a static state but a dynamic process. Life is constantly presenting you with new choices, new challenges, new opportunities to choose between the path of authenticity and the path of conformity. Each moment offers you the chance to align more deeply with your truth or to drift away from it. Alignment is a practice, a commitment, a daily choice to honor the sacred being you truly are.

Day 25: I AM Aligned

Primary Affirmation: "I AM perfectly aligned with my authentic self, my values, and my purpose."

Supporting Affirmations:

- "I AM living in harmony with my deepest truth."

- "I AM making choices that honor my authentic nature."

- "I AM expressing my unique gifts in all areas of my life."

Morning Ritual: Sit quietly and place one hand on your heart, one hand on your solar plexus (the area just below your ribcage). Breathe deeply and ask yourself: "What does alignment feel like in my body?" Notice the sensation of peace, centeredness, and wholeness that arises when you are truly connected to your authentic self. Feel this alignment as a warm, golden light flowing between your heart and your solar plexus, connecting your emotional center with your personal power center. Say aloud: "I am aligned with my truth. Every cell in my body resonates with authenticity. I move through this day in perfect harmony with who I really am."

Evening Reflection: Review your day and identify moments when you felt most aligned—times when your actions matched your values, when you felt authentic and whole, when you were expressing your true self. Also notice any moments when you felt misaligned—times when you acted against your values or suppressed your authentic nature. Without judgment, simply observe these patterns and set an intention to make more aligned choices tomorrow.

Day 26: I AM Purposeful

Primary Affirmation: "I AM living my purpose and making a meaningful contribution to the world."

Supporting Affirmations:

- "I AM clear about my unique mission and calling in life."

- "I AM using my gifts and talents to serve my highest purpose."

- "I AM making a positive difference through my authentic presence."

Morning Ritual: Write a letter to yourself from the perspective of your highest self—the version of you who is living completely aligned with your purpose. In this letter, describe what your purposeful life looks like, how you are using your gifts, what impact you are making, and how it feels to be living in complete alignment with your calling. Read this letter aloud and feel the energy of purpose filling your being. End by saying: "This is not just a dream—this is my destiny. I am already living my purpose, and it continues to unfold with perfect timing."

Evening Reflection: Identify three ways you expressed your purpose today, no matter how small. This might include helping someone, creating something beautiful, solving a problem, sharing your wisdom, or simply being a loving presence in the world. Recognize that purpose is not just about grand gestures—it is about bringing your authentic gifts to whatever you do.

Day 27: I AM Authentic

Primary Affirmation: "I AM authentic in all my relationships and interactions, honoring my truth with courage and love."

Supporting Affirmations:

- "I AM comfortable being myself in any situation or circumstance."

- "I AM expressing my honest thoughts and feelings with kindness and clarity."

- "I AM attracting people who appreciate and support my authentic self."

Morning Ritual: Stand in front of a mirror and have an honest conversation with yourself about any areas of your life where you have been hiding your true nature or pretending to be someone you're not. This might be in relationships, work, family dynamics, or social situations. Without judgment, acknowledge these areas with compassion, understanding that hiding parts of yourself was once a survival strategy. Now, commit to gradually revealing more of your authentic self in these situations. Say aloud: "I give myself permission to be real, to be human, to be authentically me. My truth is a gift to the world, and I share it with love and courage."

Evening Reflection: Write about a time when being authentic required courage—when you had to choose between being real and being liked, between expressing your truth and maintaining the status quo. How did it feel to choose authenticity? What was the outcome? Use this reflection to build your confidence in the power and beauty of living authentically.

Day 28: I AM Integrated

Primary Affirmation: "I AM a whole, integrated being, honoring all aspects of my nature with love and acceptance."

Supporting Affirmations:

- "I AM embracing both my light and my shadow with compassion."

- "I AM bringing all parts of myself into harmony and wholeness."

- "I AM comfortable with the full spectrum of my human experience."

Morning Ritual: Visualize yourself as a beautiful kaleidoscope, made up of many different colored pieces—your strengths and weaknesses, your joy and sorrow, your confidence and vulnerability, your successes and failures, your dreams and fears. See how all these pieces, when brought together, create a stunning, unique pattern that is constantly shifting and evolving but always beautiful. Embrace every aspect of yourself as necessary and valuable to the whole. Say aloud: "I am not just my light—I am also my shadow. I am not just my strengths—I am also my areas of growth. I am not just my joy—I am also my sorrows. All of me is worthy of love, and all of me contributes to my wholeness."

Evening Reflection: Think of an aspect of yourself that you have been trying to hide, fix, or eliminate—perhaps a personality trait, an emotional pattern, or a part of your history. Write a letter of acceptance to this part of yourself, acknowledging its positive intention and finding ways to honor it as part of your integrated wholeness. Commit to bringing more self-compassion to all aspects of your being.

The Psychology of Alignment

I have learned that alignment is not just a spiritual concept—it is a psychological state that can be measured and cultivated through specific practices and awareness. Psychological research has shown that people who live in alignment with their values and authentic selves report higher levels of life satisfaction, better mental health, and greater resilience in the face of challenges.

The process of alignment involves what psychologists call "congruence"—the harmony between your ideal self (who you want to be), your actual self (who you are), and your ought self (who you think you should be). When these three aspects of identity are in harmony, you experience a sense of integrity and wholeness that contributes significantly to psychological well-being.

Misalignment, on the other hand, creates what researchers call "cognitive dissonance"—the uncomfortable tension that arises when your beliefs, values, and actions are in conflict. This dissonance manifests as anxiety, depression, fatigue, and a general sense of being "off" or disconnected from yourself. The greater the misalignment, the greater the psychological distress.

The practice of self-awareness is crucial to achieving alignment because you cannot align with your truth if you don't know what your truth is. Regular self-reflection, meditation, journaling, and honest self-examination help you identify your core values, recognize your authentic desires, and understand your unique purpose and gifts.

Mindfulness practices are also essential for alignment because they help you notice when you are drifting away from your center and make conscious course corrections. When you are mindful, you can catch yourself in moments of misalignment and choose to return to authenticity rather than continuing to drift further from your truth.

The Spiritual Journey of Alignment

Still, I rise in the understanding that true alignment is ultimately a spiritual journey—a process of remembering who you really are beneath all the layers of conditioning, expectations, and false identities you have accumulated over the years. It is about returning to your divine nature, your original essence, your soul's true expression.

This spiritual dimension of alignment requires surrendering the ego's need to be special, different, or better than others and embracing the deeper truth that you are perfect exactly as you are while also being in a constant state of growth and evolution. It requires releasing attachment to how you think your life should look and trusting that your authentic path, even if it seems unconventional, is perfectly designed for your soul's development.

Prayer and meditation are powerful tools for alignment because they connect you with your higher self and divine guidance. When you take time to be still and listen to the wisdom within, you receive clarity about your next steps, insight about your purpose, and confirmation of your authentic path. This divine guidance is always available to you—you need only create the space to receive it.

Your relationship with God or the Divine is central to your alignment because when you know you are beloved, supported, and guided by infinite love, you have the courage to be authentically yourself even when it is difficult or unpopular. You know that your worth is not dependent on others' approval and that your path is valid even if others don't understand it.

The Anatomy of Misalignment

As you journey through Days 25-28, you may become more aware of areas in your life where you have been living out of alignment. Understanding the common patterns of misalignment can help you recognize and address them with compassion:

People-Pleasing: Saying yes when you mean no, suppressing your needs to meet others' expectations, and losing yourself in the attempt to be liked or accepted. Antidote: Practice setting loving boundaries and honoring your own needs as much as you honor others'.

Perfectionism: Trying to be flawless rather than authentic, hiding your struggles and weaknesses, and measuring your worth by your performance. Antidote: Embrace your humanity, share your imperfections, and define success as authenticity rather than perfection.

External Validation Seeking: Making decisions based on what will impress others rather than what feels right to you, comparing yourself to others, and measuring your worth by external achievements. Antidote: Develop internal validation skills and make choices based on your own values and desires.

Ignoring Your Intuition: Overriding your inner knowing with logical analysis, dismissing your gut feelings, and making decisions based on what you think you should do rather than what feels right. Antidote: Practice listening to and trusting your intuitive wisdom, even when it doesn't make logical sense.

Living Someone Else's Dream: Pursuing goals that belong to your parents, society, or peer group rather than your own authentic desires. Antidote: Get clear on what you actually want, not what you think you should want, and have the courage to pursue your own path.

Spiritual Bypassing: Using spiritual concepts to avoid dealing with practical realities or emotional healing, pretending to be more evolved than you are, and judging others for being "less conscious." Antidote: Embrace your humanity, do the work of healing and growth, and meet others where they are with compassion.

The Practice of Conscious Living

I have learned that alignment is not something you achieve once and then maintain effortlessly—it requires conscious, ongoing attention and choice. Every day presents opportunities to align more deeply with your truth or to drift away from it. The key is developing the awareness to recognize these choice points and the courage to consistently choose authenticity.

This practice of conscious living involves regularly checking in with yourself to assess your level of alignment. Are your daily activities reflecting your values? Are your relationships supporting your authentic self? Are your goals aligned with your soul's desires? Are you expressing your gifts in meaningful ways? Are you living with integrity and purpose?

When you notice areas of misalignment, the response is not self-judgment but loving course correction. Misalignment is not failure—it is information. It tells you where you need to make adjustments, what conversations you need to have, what boundaries you need to set, or what changes you need to make.

The practice also involves cultivating what I call "authentic courage"—the willingness to be real even when it's uncomfortable, to speak your truth even when your voice shakes, to make choices that honor your values even when they're unpopular, and to trust your path even when others question it.

The Ripple Effect of Aligned Living

When you live in true alignment, it creates waves of authenticity and inspiration that extend far beyond your personal life. Your children learn to honor their own truth when they see you honoring yours. Your friends and colleagues are inspired to live more authentically when they witness your courage to be real. Your community benefits from your unique contributions when you are expressing your authentic gifts.

Aligned people create aligned communities, and aligned communities create positive change in the world. When you are living your truth, you are not just serving your own happiness—you are serving the collective healing and evolution of humanity. Your authenticity gives others permission to be authentic too, creating a ripple effect of truth and freedom that extends far beyond what you can see.

This is the beautiful responsibility of aligned living—it is not just about your personal fulfillment but about your contribution to the greater good. When you live your truth, you are not being selfish—you are being of service to the world by offering your unique gifts and perspective.

The Courage to Be Different

I have learned that living in alignment often requires the courage to be different, to walk a path that others may not understand, to make choices that seem unconventional or risky. It requires trusting your inner guidance even when it contradicts external advice, following your passion even when it doesn't make financial sense, and honoring your values even when it costs you opportunities or relationships.

This courage to be different is not about being rebellious or contrarian—it is about being faithful to your authentic self. It is about recognizing that you were not created to be a copy of someone else but to be an original expression of divine creativity. Your differences are not flaws to be corrected but gifts to be celebrated.

When you have the courage to be authentically different, you often discover that what makes you unique is exactly what the world needs. Your unconventional perspective, your unusual combination of gifts, your distinctive way of seeing and being—these are not accidents but purposeful aspects of your design that enable you to make contributions that no one else can make.

Integration as a Daily Practice

Living in alignment is not about making one big decision and then coasting—it is about making countless small decisions every day to honor your truth, express your authenticity, and choose integrity. It is about integrating all aspects of your life so that there is coherence between your inner world and your outer world.

This integration involves bringing your spiritual values into your work life, your professional skills into your personal relationships, your creative gifts into practical endeavors, and your authentic self into every interaction. It means refusing to compartmentalize your life and instead living as a whole, integrated being.

The practice of integration also involves regularly reassessing your life to ensure it continues to reflect your evolving truth. As you grow and change, your expression of alignment may also evolve. What served your authentic self five years ago may no longer fit who you are becoming. Alignment is not rigid—it is fluid and responsive to your ongoing growth and development.

The Promise of Authentic Living

And so, dear reader, as you complete Days 25-28 of your transformation journey, know that you have stepped fully into the power and beauty of aligned living. You have remembered who you truly are beneath all the masks and personas you have worn. You have reclaimed your right to be authentic, purposeful, and whole.

The final phase of your journey will build upon this foundation of alignment as you step into your unstoppable nature. But all that is to come will be grounded in the truth you are claiming now—the deep knowing that you are meant to live as your authentic self, to express your unique gifts, and to contribute your distinctive light to the world.

Still, you rise, not because you need to prove anything to anyone, but because you are ready to live as the aligned, authentic, purposeful being you have always been meant to be. The light finds you, steady and sure, and in that light, you see the integrated, whole, magnificently authentic person you truly are.

Grace finds you here, in this moment of recognition, in this claiming of your authentic power, in this homecoming to your true self. You are aligned. You have always been whole. And now, finally, you are ready to live like you believe it.

Grace finds us when we finally have the courage to stop trying to be someone else's version of perfect and start being our own version of authentic.

CHAPTER 8

~~~

Your Radiant Future - I AM Unstoppable

Days 29-30: Maintaining Momentum and Expanding Your Vision

There is a sacred fire that burns within every soul, a flame that cannot be extinguished by circumstances, diminished by setbacks, or dulled by the passing of time. I have felt this fire blazing in my own heart, have watched it grow from a flickering ember of hope into an inferno of unstoppable purpose, and I have learned that this divine spark is not reserved for the chosen few—it lives within every human being, waiting to be fanned into the full flame of their magnificent potential.

You are unstoppable. Not because you are invincible or immune to challenges, but because you have discovered the unshakeable truth of who you are—a being of infinite worth, unlimited potential, abundant supply, unshakeable confidence, indomitable resilience, magnetic attraction, and perfect alignment with your divine purpose. You are unstoppable because you have remembered that every seeming obstacle is actually a stepping stone, every apparent ending is actually a new beginning, and every moment of doubt is actually an invitation to choose faith once again.

I have learned that being unstoppable is not about never falling down—it is about always getting back up. It is not about never feeling fear—it is about feeling the fear and moving forward anyway. It is not about having all the answers—it is about having the faith to take the next step even when the path ahead is unclear. You are unstoppable because your connection to the Divine is unbreakable, your purpose is unchangeable, and your light is unquenchable.

The Nature of Unstoppable Force

For too long, we have confused being unstoppable with being hard, aggressive, or relentless in a forceful way. But I have learned that true unstoppable force is more like water—soft yet persistent, gentle yet powerful, yielding yet ultimately victorious. Water does not fight the rock; it simply keeps flowing around it, over it, through it, until eventually the rock is worn smooth or carved into something beautiful.

True unstoppable force comes not from pushing against resistance but from flowing with purpose, not from fighting obstacles but from transforming them, not from demanding that life conform to your will but from aligning your will with the highest good and trusting that the universe will move mountains to support your aligned action.

When you are truly unstoppable, you do not need to announce it or prove it to anyone. Your unstoppable nature is evident in your calm persistence, your quiet confidence, your unwavering faith, and your ability to keep moving forward even when progress seems slow or invisible. You are unstoppable because you know that every step counts, every effort matters, and every moment of choosing love over fear, hope over despair, and faith over doubt is a victory in itself.

Still, I rise in the knowing that being unstoppable is not a destination but a decision—a choice you make again and again, day after day, moment by moment. It is the decision to believe in yourself when others doubt you, to keep going when you feel like quitting, to find another way when the first path is blocked, and to trust in your ultimate victory even when current circumstances suggest otherwise.

Day 29: I AM Unstoppable

Primary Affirmation: "I AM unstoppable in my pursuit of my dreams, my purpose, and my highest good."

Supporting Affirmations:

- "I AM persistent, determined, and unwavering in my commitment to my goals."

- "I AM overcoming every obstacle with grace, wisdom, and creative solutions."

- "I AM moving forward with confidence, knowing that nothing can permanently stop me."

Morning Ritual: Visualize yourself as a river flowing toward the ocean—your ultimate destination, your fulfilled purpose, your realized dreams. See how the river never stops flowing, no matter what obstacles it encounters. When it meets a boulder, it flows around it. When it faces a cliff, it becomes a waterfall. When it reaches a dam, it rises until it flows over the top. Feel this same flowing, persistent energy within yourself. Place your hands over your heart and feel the unstoppable force of your life energy, your purpose, your divine mission. Say aloud: "I am like this river—unstoppable, persistent, always finding a way. No obstacle can permanently block my path because I am connected to an infinite source of power, creativity, and determination."

Evening Reflection: Write about a time in your life when you were unstoppable—when you persisted despite obstacles, when you found a way when there seemed to be no way, when you kept going even when others gave up. What inner resources did you draw upon? What beliefs sustained you? How can you apply this same unstoppable energy to your current dreams and goals? Celebrate your proven track record of persistence and determination.

Day 30: I AM Victorious

Primary Affirmation: "I AM victorious in all my endeavors, celebrating my wins and learning from every experience."

Supporting Affirmations:

- "I AM already successful and continue to achieve greater victories every day."

- "I AM grateful for how far I have come and excited about where I am going."

- "I AM living proof that dreams come true when you combine faith with action."

Morning Ritual: Create a "Victory Crown" ceremony. This can be an actual crown, a special hat, or simply the gesture of placing your hands on your head. As you place this crown upon your head, declare yourself victorious—not because your journey is over, but because you have already won the most important victory: the victory over limiting beliefs, the victory over fear, the victory over the voice that says you are not enough. You have completed 30 days of transformation, and that alone makes you victorious. Say aloud: "I crown myself victorious. I have conquered doubt, overcome limitation, and stepped into the fullness of who I was meant to be. I am victorious today, and I will be victorious tomorrow, because victory is my natural state."

Evening Reflection: Write a letter to yourself celebrating the transformation you have experienced over these 30 days. Acknowledge the growth you have made, the fears you have faced, the beliefs you have changed, and the person you have become. Include specific examples of how you have embodied each of the "I AM" affirmations: enough, unlimited, abundant, confident, resilient, magnetic, aligned, and unstoppable. End the letter by making a commitment to continue this journey of growth and transformation for the rest of your life.

The Science of Unstoppable Momentum

I have learned that being unstoppable is not just a mindset—it is a scientifically observable phenomenon that can be cultivated through specific practices and principles. Physics teaches us about momentum—the tendency of a body in motion to stay in motion unless acted upon by an external force. The same principle applies to human achievement and personal transformation.

Neuroscience has shown that success breeds success through the release of dopamine, the neurotransmitter associated with reward and motivation. Each time you achieve a goal, no matter how small, your brain releases dopamine, which reinforces the neural pathways associated with success and makes you more likely to take action toward future goals. This creates a positive feedback loop that builds unstoppable momentum over time.

The practice of celebrating small wins—which has been woven throughout these 30 days—is crucial for building this neurochemical momentum. When you acknowledge and appreciate your progress, you are literally training your brain to expect success and to seek out more opportunities for achievement. This is why unstoppable people often seem to have "lucky breaks"—they have trained their brains to notice and act on opportunities that others miss.

Research in positive psychology has also revealed the power of what psychologists call "learned optimism"—the ability to interpret challenges as temporary, specific, and surmountable rather than permanent, pervasive, and insurmountable. Unstoppable people have learned to reframe setbacks as setups for comeback, to see obstacles as opportunities for creative problem-solving, and to view failures as valuable feedback rather than final verdicts.

The practice of visualization, which has been central to your 30-day journey, literally rewires your brain for success. When you repeatedly visualize yourself achieving your goals, your brain creates neural pathways as if you had already experienced that success. This makes the actual achievement feel familiar and attainable rather than foreign and impossible.

The Spiritual Foundation of Victory

Still, I rise in the understanding that true unstoppable force is not self-generated but God-generated. It comes from aligning with the infinite power of Divine love and allowing that power to flow through you in service of your highest purpose. When you know that you are not working alone but in partnership with the creative force of the universe, you become truly unstoppable because you have access to unlimited resources, infinite wisdom, and eternal support.

This spiritual foundation of unstoppable force requires what I call "surrendered determination"—the ability to work with passionate commitment while holding your goals lightly, to pursue your dreams with dedication while trusting in divine timing, and to give your all while surrendering the outcomes to God. This paradoxical balance of effort and surrender is what makes spiritual warriors truly unstoppable.

Prayer and meditation are not passive activities for unstoppable people—they are the source of their power. In the stillness of communion with the Divine, you receive the guidance, strength, and inspiration needed to take your next steps. You are reminded that your dreams are not just personal desires but divine assignments, that your success serves not just your own happiness but the greater good of all.

Your relationship with God is what makes you unstoppable because it provides an unshakeable foundation that external circumstances cannot touch. When you know you are beloved, guided, and empowered by infinite love, you can face any challenge with confidence, navigate any obstacle with wisdom, and persist through any difficulty with grace.

The Evolution of Your Identity

Over these 30 days, you have undergone a profound transformation of identity. You began as someone who may have doubted their worth, questioned their potential, worried about scarcity, lacked confidence, struggled with setbacks, chased after what they wanted, felt fragmented and confused about their purpose, and sometimes felt like giving up.

You are ending as someone who knows they are enough, believes in their unlimited potential, lives from abundance consciousness, embodies unshakeable confidence, transforms obstacles into opportunities, attracts their desires with magnetic force, lives in alignment with their authentic purpose, and has become unstoppable in their pursuit of their highest good.

This transformation of identity is the most powerful change that can occur in a human life because identity determines behavior, behavior determines results, and results determine your reality. By changing who you believe yourself to be at the deepest level, you have changed what you believe is possible for your life, and this changed belief will manifest as changed circumstances in ways that will continue to unfold for years to come.

The beautiful truth is that this new identity is not something you have created but something you have remembered. You have not become someone new—you have uncovered who you have always been beneath the layers of conditioning, fear, and false beliefs. This is why the transformation feels so natural and right—because you are not pretending to be someone else; you are finally being yourself.

Maintaining Your Transformation

As you complete these 30 days, you may wonder how to maintain the momentum and continue the growth you have experienced. I want to share with you the principles that will help you not only maintain your transformation but continue expanding into even greater versions of yourself:

Daily Affirmation Practice: Continue speaking your "I AM" statements every day. These affirmations are not just for the 30-day program—they are tools for lifelong transformation. Choose one or two that resonate most deeply with you and make them part of your daily spiritual practice.

Regular Self-Reflection: Set aside time each week to reflect on your growth, celebrate your progress, and identify areas where you want to continue expanding. Growth is not a one-time event but a lifelong journey of becoming.

Consistent Action: Continue taking inspired action toward your dreams and goals. Transformation is not just about changing your thoughts—it is about changing your actions and your life. Let your new identity express itself through new choices and behaviors.

Community and Support: Surround yourself with people who support your growth and share your commitment to living at a higher level. The company you keep has a profound influence on who you become and what you achieve.

Continued Learning: Keep reading books, listening to podcasts, attending workshops, and engaging with content that supports your continued growth and expansion. Your mind is like a garden—it will grow whatever you plant in it.

Service to Others: Use your transformation to help others transform. Share your story, offer encouragement, and be a living example of what is possible when someone commits to growing into their highest potential.

The Ripple Effect of Your Transformation

Your transformation over these 30 days has created ripples that extend far beyond your personal life. Every time you chose faith over fear, every time you spoke your worth into existence, every time you acted from abundance rather than scarcity, every time you embodied confidence instead of doubt, every time you turned obstacles into opportunities, every time you attracted good into your life, every time you lived authentically, and every time you refused to give up, you were not just changing yourself—you were contributing to the positive transformation of the world.

Your children, if you have them, will benefit from having a parent who models self-worth, unlimited thinking, abundant living, genuine confidence, resilience, magnetic attraction, authentic living, and unstoppable determination. Your friends and colleagues will be inspired by your example to examine their own beliefs and possibilities. Your community will benefit from your increased capacity to contribute, serve, and create positive change.

This is the beautiful responsibility of personal transformation—it is never just personal. When you rise, you lift others. When you heal, you contribute to collective healing. When you grow, you expand the realm of possibility for everyone whose life you touch. Your transformation is your gift to the world.

The Continuing Journey

I want you to understand that completing these 30 days is not the end of your journey—it is the beginning of your life as a fully empowered, consciously creating, divinely aligned human being. You have built a foundation of unshakeable self-worth, unlimited potential, abundant consciousness, genuine confidence, indomitable resilience, magnetic attraction, authentic alignment, and unstoppable determination. Now the real adventure begins.

From this foundation, you will continue to grow, create, contribute, and become. You will face new challenges, but you will meet them with the strength you have cultivated. You will encounter new opportunities, and you will seize them with the confidence you have developed. You will experience setbacks, but you will bounce back with the resilience you have built. You will have new dreams, and you will attract them with the magnetic power you have awakened.

The person you have become through this 30-day journey is not a role you are playing or a mask you are wearing—it is the authentic you, the real you, the you that you have always been beneath the surface. This is who you are, and this is who you will continue to be as you move forward into the magnificent future that awaits you.

Your Declaration of Unstoppable Living

And so, dear reader, as you stand at the completion of this 30-day transformation journey, I invite you to make a declaration—not to me, not to the world, but to yourself and to the Divine force that lives within you. This is your declaration of who you are and how you will live from this day forward:

"I AM enough, exactly as I am, and I will never again allow anyone or anything to convince me otherwise. I AM unlimited in my potential, and I will not let fear or doubt constrain my dreams. I AM abundant in all areas of my life, and I will live from overflow rather than scarcity. I AM confident in my abilities and my worth, and I will not shrink to make others comfortable. I AM resilient and can handle whatever life brings my way with grace and strength. I AM magnetic and naturally attract everything that serves my highest good. I AM aligned with my authentic self and my divine purpose, and I will not compromise my truth for anyone's approval. I AM unstoppable in my pursuit of my dreams, and I will never give up on myself or my vision.

I declare that this is who I am, this is how I will live, and this is the legacy I will leave. I rise not because I have to, but because I choose to. I shine not because it's easy, but because the world needs my light. I love not because I'm perfect, but because love is who I am."

Still, you rise, not as someone who has reached the end of their journey, but as someone who has just begun to live the life they were always meant to live. The light finds you, steady and sure, and in that light, you see not just who you have been or who you are, but who you are becoming—an unstoppable force of love, light, and purpose in this world.

Grace finds you here, in this moment of completion that is also a commencement, in this ending that is also a beginning, in this transformation that is actually a homecoming to your truest self. You are unstoppable. You have always been unstoppable. And now, finally, you are ready to live like you believe it.

Grace finds us when we finally understand that we were never meant to be stoppable, that our light was always meant to shine, and that our victory was assured before we ever took our first breath.

CONCLUSION

Your New Beginning

There is a moment when the caterpillar, having completed its mysterious transformation in the darkness of the cocoon, feels the first crack in its protective shell. Something deeper calls—a knowing that it was not meant to stay hidden but to emerge, to spread wings it has never used, to soar in skies it has only imagined. Today, dear reader, you stand at that sacred threshold, no longer the person who began this journey thirty days ago, but ready to embrace the magnificent being you have become.

For thirty days, you have spoken new life into your existence. You have declared your worth, claimed your unlimited nature, embodied abundance, stood in confidence, risen resilient, magnetized your desires, aligned with your truth, and become unstoppable. You have done more than complete a 30-day program—you have undergone a profound metamorphosis of spirit, mind, and heart.

The Sacred Journey You Have Traveled

Thirty days ago, you may have awakened to mornings filled with self-doubt and uncertainty. Perhaps you looked in the mirror and saw someone lacking or limited. But day by day, affirmation by affirmation, you have rewoven the fabric of your identity. You have replaced the threads of limitation with strands of possibility, exchanged the colors of scarcity for the hues of abundance, traded the patterns of fear for the designs of faith.

This transformation happened because you showed up, even when you didn't feel like it. You spoke words of truth even when they felt foreign. You chose to believe in possibilities even when reality suggested otherwise. You had the courage to become who you were always meant to be.

The Science and Spirit of Transformation

What you have accomplished is both neurological and spiritual. Every affirmation has literally rewired your brain. The neural pathways that once fired thoughts of inadequacy have been weakened, while new pathways of self-worth and confidence have been strengthened. Your brain now automatically seeks evidence of your capabilities rather than your limitations.

But this is far more than brain training—it is spiritual awakening. You have remembered who you truly are beneath all the conditioning and false beliefs. You have reconnected with the divine spark that has always lived within you. You are not just someone who has learned new techniques—you are a beloved child of God who has finally accepted your place in the cosmic family of love.

Living Your New Reality

Now comes the most important part—living from your new reality. The affirmations you have spoken are declarations of who you are and how you will move through the world from this day forward. The identity you have cultivated is your authentic self, finally free to express its truth.

Living from your new reality means making decisions from your worth rather than your wounds, choosing opportunities that align with your unlimited nature, and managing resources from abundance consciousness. It means approaching challenges with confidence, bouncing back with resilience, attracting through magnetic authenticity, and persisting with unstoppable determination.

When you notice yourself slipping into old patterns, simply return to your affirmations, reconnect with your truth, and choose again. Each moment offers a fresh opportunity to embody your new identity.

Your Sacred Responsibility

With transformation comes responsibility. You now carry the light of possibility and the power of authentic living. Your sacred responsibility is to continue growing, to keep shining, to never dim your light to make others comfortable. You are to use your gifts in service of the greater good and be a beacon of hope for those still finding their way.

Your life becomes your message. Your example becomes your teaching. Your transformation becomes your gift to a world that needs to see that change is possible, that people can heal, and that miracles happen to those who have the courage to believe in themselves.

The Promise Within You

As you close this book, I leave you with a promise that lives within you: You promise to never again accept less than you deserve or make yourself small. You promise to continue growing and keep your heart open to love, your mind open to possibility, and your spirit open to divine guidance.

You promise to remember, always and forever, that you are enough, unlimited, abundant, confident, resilient, magnetic, aligned, and unstoppable. Not because you have achieved these states perfectly, but because they are the truth of who you are at your core—the reality of your divine nature.

Your New Dawn

The sun rises on your transformed life, revealing a landscape of infinite possibility. You see now that every dream you have ever held is not only possible but probable when you approach it from who you have become. The limitations you once accepted were never real—they were only beliefs, and beliefs can be changed.

Still, you rise—not because the journey is over but because it has truly begun. You rise because you now know who you are and whose you are. You rise because your light was meant to shine, your voice was meant to be heard, and your love was meant to heal the world.

Grace finds you here, in this moment of completion that is also commencement. You are no longer becoming—you have become. You are no longer seeking—you have found. You are no longer hoping—you are knowing.

Your "I AM" is no longer a question—it is a declaration, a celebration, a foundation upon which you will build the rest of your extraordinary life.

Welcome to your new beginning. Welcome to your transformed life. Welcome home to yourself.

Grace finds us when we finally understand that we were never broken and needed to be fixed—we were always whole and needed only to remember.

HAVE SOMETHING TO SHARE?

I'd love to hear from you! Whether this book spoke to your soul, inspired a new way of thinking, or sparked fresh questions, your voice is part of the journey. Please connect on Facebook https://www.facebook.com/mindfulplains share your thoughts, leave a comment and join the conversation. Your feedback helps me grow as a writer and supports others along their path. Don't forget to follow our page for updates, new releases and a little extra inspiration. Let's keep walking this beautiful journey - together.

— Harmony Ziba

Thank you 🙏 💜

AUTHOR PROFILE

Harmony Ziba is a transformational author and spiritual guide whose powerful words touch thousands of souls across the globe. Drawing from her own journey of overcoming adversity and discovering her divine worth, Harmony writes with the lyrical grace and profound wisdom that comes from walking through darkness and choosing to rise toward the light.

Her writing style weaves together poetic storytelling, practical spirituality and deep emotional truth, creating experiences that don't just inform but transform. Harmony believes that every person carries within them an unlimited capacity for growth, abundance, and authentic joy - her books serve as gentle yet powerful guides for remembering these truths.

When she's not writing, Harmony finds inspiration in nature's quiet moments, meaningful conversations with fellow seekers, and the daily miracle of ordinary people choosing extraordinary courage. She lives with an unshakeable faith that transformation is always possible, and that every reader who picks up her books is exactly where they need to be to begin their own journey home to themselves.

Printed in Dunstable, United Kingdom

66888370R00077